15 BEST Airport Restaurants

plus 2,347 Runner-ups

By

John F. Purner

Table of Contents

Foreword	**3**
Introduction	**5**
15 Best	**7**
2,347 Runner-Ups	**12**

15 Best Airport Restaurants

Foreword

I began traveling seriously decades ago. With a promotion had come a new role. I had always wanted to be, a salesman and suddenly I was. My travel was by air and the products I sold were mainframe computers not socks. Those two things at least separated me from the life of Arthur Miller's, Willy Loman in his classic tale, **"Death of a Salesman"**.

It was 1972. Air travel was gracious and the company I worked for generous. I traveled the skies of the southeast with a magic device called an Air Travel Card, it purchased First Class passage for me (*I said it was a generous company*) with all of the airlines of that day. I was privileged to be a subscriber to the **OAG** (Official Air Travel Guide). It gave me the airlines' schedules so I could plan my trips which were usually "spur of the moment" happenings.

Typically, I would set an appointment with a faraway prospect for a meeting the next day or later in the week. Then I would pack and go to the airport after checking flight schedules in the **OAG**. There was no Internet and no World Wide Web and none was required. I simply told the airline counter representative my destination, airline and flight number. She then wrote out, by hand, my ticket and charged it to my air travel card. There were no special deals in those days; all fares were the same within class. It didn't matter when you booked, the price was the same.

Passengers dressed in their Sunday best. All bags were checked as no one would think of carrying a suitcase on board, briefcases certainly but suitcases NEVER! Once aboard, the stewardess in the First Class cabin took drink orders and passed out cigarettes and playing cards after hanging up every gentleman's coat jacket on a hangar and placing it neatly into the front cabin's closet. Cocktails were mixed with spirits flowing from freshly opened bottles. At the end of each trip, the partially used bottles were offered to passengers or thrown away if no one wanted to be bothered with carting away the free liquor.

The food service was perfect. I recall a wonderfully prepared and piping hot standing roast beef being wheeled on a serving cart into the center aisle. The stewardess then approached each passenger in turn to ascertain which cut they preferred and how much they would like. Their portion was placed on a china plate; fresh vegetables were ladled beside them. It was then placed a miniature white table cloth which covered the fold away tray table. Amazing desserts were presented for the end of the meal and then fruit and cheese, brandy if you liked. Life was good, very, very good. The airlines did all of this because it was the only way they had to differentiate themselves. The routes and schedules were set by the government as were the fares. All that was left was service and frills.

15 Best Airport Restaurants

The golden age of air travel died with the election of James Earl Carter to the Presidency of the United States of America. He and his Secretary of Transportation Alfred Kahn had an economic theory that they felt would increase competition, lower fares and open air travel to the masses. Its principle feature was de-regulation. The airlines not the government would set routes, schedules and fares. Anyone who wanted to start an airline could. The certification process was a snap. The Carter administration did the same thing to trucking. I am not making a political comment or a judgment I am presenting a historical fact; rather like saying Abraham Lincoln was the 16th President of the USA. All human actions have consequences some of which are unintended. It seems to always be those unintended consequences that most affect our lives. So it was in this case.

Within hours of implementation things changed BIG TIME. All airline advertising touted low prices not high quality. Food service declined in favor of cost cutting. Lower fares brought hoards of new air travelers. Prior to 1974 only 4% of the American population had ever traveled by air. Today the number has reversed; less than 4% of the American population has never traveled by air.

Mission accomplished? Yes and no.

Commercial air travel is certainly available and affordable but what was once a treat has become a hassle. Prior to deregulation Continental Airlines was advertised as the "Proud Bird with the Golden Tail" and each flight was accompanied by their famous, "Champagne Service". The bird's feathers were plucked and service became a memory. A smile rather than a snarl from a stewardess is today's unexpected pleasure.

Many things about air travel have changed, some for better, some forever. Anyone traveling after 1980 can quickly agree that a fresh Big Mac and a bag of fries purchased from a gate side McDonalds is far superior to the cardboard sandwiches routinely provided throughout the '80s and '90s. Airport food offerings have steadily improved while airline food service has almost completely disappeared on domestic flights.

15 Best Airport Restaurants

Introduction

Travel done well is about new discoveries and new experiences. America is a vast country divided by geography and demographics into rich regional culinary distinctions.

One of the most enjoyable pleasures travel provides is food. Leave Wichita, jet to New Orleans, order a plate of red beans and rice and you'll know very quickly that you're *"not in Kansas anymore"*.

The 15 restaurants selected for special mention in this book offer dining experiences unique to their region. Mexican food, for example, is offered in 1,000's of restaurants in hundreds of towns and cities that dot our great country but you can't get Tex-Mex outside of Texas. When you're in Texas you should not pass it up. Tex-Mex is wicked good. So is Seattle seafood.

Our winners weren't selected solely for their cuisine. One is included solely for its amazing interior design and memorable architecture. We eat with our eyes as well as our mouths.

Chain restaurants are consistent. If you like Chili's menu, presentation and food in Orlando you'll be equally pleased with it in Dallas. Our list of 2,347 runner-ups is loaded with chain restaurants. They are all good but none are unique and aren't supposed to be. Their stock and trade is no surprises. Our 15 Best list includes no national chains. Each of our selections offers a unique regional dining experience.

So why include all 2,347 runner-ups? Our air transportation system is based on a hub and spoke technique which pretty much guarantees that if you are flying commercially from city A to city B you will land, change planes and likely spend some quality time at an airport in city C, one of the hub cities. Atlanta is such a place. It has over 125 restaurants scattered across five massive terminals connected by a light rail system. Knowing which restaurants are available and which terminal hosts them can turn a disappointing layover into a happy meal memory. There are many great restaurants in our nation's hubs and many of them are part of national chains. A TGI Fridays or a Chili's is often a welcomed friend amid a sea of traveling strangers.

Restaurants change more quickly than books. Once a book is printed the information is locked in its perfectly typeset pages until the next Edition which maybe a year or more away.

We have setup a website to provide current information as a companion to this book. You may access **www.purner.com/15best.html** at no charge. Once there you'll see a clean white page with two clickable options: **"Sign Me Up!"** and **"Let Me In!"**. On your first visit click **"Sign Me Up!"** from then on just hit **"Let Me In!"**.

15 Best Airport Restaurants

The website is designed for maximum user interaction. You can update all of the restaurant information, post your positive or negative reviews and add your personal rating – one to five. Our **Traveler's Advisory** section will keep you up to date with all of the need to know information to make each trip as carefree as possible. Our **Editorial Page** will let you know what's up in the world of traveling foodies. You'll want to take a look at our **Deals on Meals** section to see what special offers airport restaurants are making to **15 Best** readers.

I hope you'll enjoy this book and that it will make air travel more pleasurable for you. If you have an overall suggestion or comments about it please write email at **best@purner.com**. I look forward to hearing from you and promise to respond.

15 Best Airport Restaurants

15 Best

Acme Oyster House   *Regional*
    New Orleans, LA
    Ticket Lobby   (504) 522-5973
    www.acmeoyster.com

Acme is a true New Orleans oyster joint and the best of them all. From 1910 until 1986 you had to go to Iberville Street in the French Quarter to dine at this shrine to seafood. Now there are five locations. Fortunately for travelers one is located in the Ticket Lobby of the Louis Armstrong International Airport. Do yourself a favor and eat here whenever you can. Grab a half dozen oysters, a bowl of seafood gumbo and my personal favorite an oyster po-boy sandwich. Be sure to tell the waiter you want it dressed. What does that mean? Ask, you might prefer it naked but he'll know you're a tourist.

Anthony's Restaurant and Fish Bar   *American*
    Seattle, WA
    Central Concourse C   206-431-3000
    www.anthonys.com

Anthony's is known for choosing the freshest premium fish and shellfish in the Northwest. The restaurant serves breakfast, lunch and dinner in a beautifully appointed dining room with runway and Olympic mountain views beyond. A wide variety of local delicacies including fresh Puget Sound oysters on the half shell, wild Alaskan King Salmon and Anthony's signature Wild Mountain Blackberry Cobbler. Anthony's is a place to enjoy a great glass of Northwest wine, microbrew or your favorite cocktail while dining with real china and silverware! All menu items can be carried on your flight.

Axel's Bonfire   *American*
    Minneapolis, MN
    Terminal Lindbergh Checkpoint 3   612-726-5360
    www.axelsbonfire.com

Axel's Bonfire breaks away from typical airport food and its Midwestern location by cooking up great American cuisine with a Southwestern flair. The menu lists rotisserie chicken, wood-fire steaks, seafood, ribs, fajitas and their famous over-sized salads. Remember this is Minnesota not Phoenix go with the **Pan-Fried Walleye** topped with toasted almonds. Your first bite will have you understanding why they are the #1 seller of walleye in Minnesota. Alex's is pricey but worth it.

Ebisu   *Japanese*
    San Francisco, CA
    International Terminal North Food Court   650-588-2549
    www.ebisusushi.com/

15 Best Airport Restaurants

For nearly 30 years Steve Fujii and his wife Koko have created a San Francisco landmark restaurant that has continued to grow and flourish. Today there are 2 **Ebisu** locations; one is at San Francisco International Airport inside the Food Court in the International Terminal.

Ebisu has surely succeeded at bringing all forms of Japanese culinary arts to the air traveler fortunate enough to be passing by their SFO location. Stop and enjoy a meal or grab n go. You'll be very glad you did. I suggest starting with a **TOOTSIE ROLL**. Unlike the favorite confection of my youth this one is made of Salmon and green onion which is deep fried, rolled and served on soybean paper. Hmmm, Hmmm Good! I usually follow-up with the Chicken Teriyaki rice bowl, a simple dish that never fails to satisfy.

Encounter Restaurant and Bar   *American*
     Los Angeles, CA
     Theme Building   (310) 215-5151
     www.encounterlax.com

At the center of Los Angeles International Airport stands the landmark Theme Building which is home to the **Encounter Restaurant and Bar**. With 135-foot high parabolic arches and a futuristic design, the unique structure is one of the most recognizable buildings in the U.S. Its design features 360 degree views of the airport.

A meal at any restaurant is primarily about the food no matter how spectacular the surroundings. **Encounter's** does not disappoint. Its menu is sprinkled with **award-winning "California Fresh" cuisine** prepared under the direction of Chef, Michel Audeon. Hours are: Lunch from 11:00 a.m. to 4:00 p.m. 7 days a week; Dinner is served from 4:00 p.m. to 9:30 p.m. Thursday, Friday, Saturday & Sunday.

Figs Restaurant   *American*
     New York (La Guardia), NY
     Terminal Central Gate Pre-Security   (718) 446-7600
     www.figslga.com

King of the mountain Chef Todd English knocked it out of the park when he opened *Figs* at La Guardia in 2000. The great food, fast and friendly service, and stylish atmosphere will make you forget you're in an airport. The cuisine is stylish Mediterranean, the wines above adequate and the service magnificent. If your flight is delayed thank your lucky stars and head immediately to *Figs*. Try the **Fig & Prosciutto** flatbread. Crispy rosemary crust with fig and balsamic jam, prosciutto and gorgonzola cheese, you'll be surprised at how good it is.

There is a miniature version of the mother ship named **Figs Café** inside Concourse D.

15 Best Airport Restaurants

Freckle's Frozen Custard   *Desserts*
    Tulsa, OK
    Food Court
    www.frecklesfrozencustard.com

Ice cream, frozen yogurt and gelato are all terrific frozen desserts. If you are lucky you can find some good examples during your travels. If you have never had Frozen Custard you are in for a treat. It is three levels above supper premium ice creams. It has to do with the way it is made. The best frozen custard in the world can be found at the Tulsa Airport. It is made fresh daily and each day there is a flavor of the day. Order it!!! You be amazed. I'm not much of a dessert guy but this is worth the trip. **Freckle's** has won every award for culinary excellence that is available in its region.

Gallagher's Steakhouse   *American*
    New York, (Newark), NY
    Terminal C Gate 3   973-286-0034
    www.gallaghersnysteakhouse.com

For 80 years, people have flocked to **Gallagher's** for a perfect steak. Only USDA Prime Beef, dry aged for 21 days at a constant temperature of 36 degrees is used. This all-natural process ensures tenderness. Next they toss it on a grill fired with hickory coals. Finally, they serve it to lucky you. Legendary restaurateur Jerome Brody works hard to make certain that is formula is meticulously followed. This is a place to sit and enjoy, it is not grab and go fare.

Harry Caray's Seventh Inning Stretch   *American*
    Chicago, IL (Midway)
    Triangle   773-948-6300
    www.harrycarays.com/seventh_inning_stretch.html

The only full service restaurant and bar at Chicago's Midway Airport. A combination of mahogany paneling, mosaic tile and a veritable museum of baseball history create a warm and casual elegance. **Harry Caray's Seventh Inning Stretch** is perfect for those looking to have a great meal at a premier Chicago restaurant without leaving the airport. It is ideal for travelers looking to take a freshly made sandwich to their flight. For a lunch or dinner entrée order the **Harry's Boneless Chicken Vesuvio** and finish with a slice of **Eli's Turtle Cheesecake**. If you're in for breakfast stake your claim on the **French Toast** with a side of applewood smoked bacon. Everything on the menu can be packed for your flight if you prefer to fly-dine.

Ivar's Seafood Bar   *Seafood*
    Seattle, WA
    Pacific Market Place   206-248-0012
    www.ivars.net

15 Best Airport Restaurants

Ivar's was born in 1938 and has been a Seattle attraction ever since. They feature classic Northwest seafood based on the original recipes of founder, Ivar Haglund. You'll find fresh fish grilled to perfection including Alaskan deep water halibut, salmon and Pacific cod. **Ivar's** famous clam chowder and fish n' chips are my personal favorites! If you're rushing for a flight this is a **GREAT** grab-n-go.

Legal C Bar *American*
    Boston, MA
    Terminal C   857-241-2000
    www.legalseafoods.com

Legal Sea Food is one of New England's finest purveyors of the fruits of the sea. Lucky for those of us who ply the New England skies, they have three locations at Boston's Logan Airport. **Legal Sea Foods** "C" fare includes clams, cod, crab and chowder as well as custom cocktails. The restaurant's amenities include luggage cubbies, many outlets for electronic devices and communal seating for single travelers seeking companionship. Don't overlook the **Portuguese Fisherman's Stew**. It is a delightful blend of whitefish stewed with mussels, clams and chouriço sausage in a saffron tomato broth. That said my favorite is the **Lobster Roll** made of freshly shucked lobster, celery and mayo spread on a brioche roll.

Obrycki's Restaurant and Bar *Seafood*
    Baltimore, MD
    Terminal B Gate 9   410-732-6399
    www.obryckis.com/BWI_info_W8.cfm

It's really all about the crab cakes. **Obrycki's** has been turning 'em out in Baltimore sense 1944. What to order? Start with a bowl of crab soup and then enjoy a Crab Cake sandwich. It's a bargain. What about breakfast? Crab cakes and eggs of course. There are other's that serve seafood at this airport and they are good also, **Obrycki's** is simply better. When my schedule requires a visit to Washington DC I demand to fly into and out of nearby Baltimore so I can enjoy this restaurant. It is a great regional find.

Pappasito's *Mexican*
    Houston (Hobby), TX
    Terminal Central Concourse   281-657-6157
    www.pappasitos.com/location/?id=59

If you haven't sampled Tex-Mex your foodie status is seriously lacking! **Pappasito's** has some of the best I've found. You can dine in or grab 'n go either way you'll be well served. My favorite dish has long been the cheese enchiladas. I never grab and go though because I like to wash them down with a tasty margarita. There are two **Pappasito's** secrets you need to

15 Best Airport Restaurants

remember. Breakfast service begins at 5:00am and they have **FREE** Wifi Internet.

Paschal's Southern Delights   *Regional*
    Atlanta, GA
    Terminal C Centerpoint   404-209-8335
    Terminal A Centerpoint   404-209-1757
    Atrium SE   404-761-4160
    www.paschalsatlanta.com

Paschal's isn't just a restaurant it has been an Atlanta institution since 1947. Some call their cuisine Southern Soul food. I call it home cooking, you'll cal it amazing. I usually order the fired chicken or the pot roast, sometimes both. Combine either with a sampling from their extensive list of vegetables and corn bread and you're good to go. Don't you dare walk away without trying the Peach Cobbler! It deserves its worldwide fame.

Rosario's Cantina   *Mexican*
    San Antonio, TX
    Terminal 2   210-826-3282
    www.rosariossa.com

For nearly two decades, **Rosario's Mexican Café y Cantina** has been the dining draw for the Southtown-King William area of San Antonio. Here's all you need to know. The award winning and highly respected *Texas Monthly* magazine, named **Rosario's** Grilled Fish or Shrimp Taco as the No. 2 dish **"You Must Eat before You Die"**. I agree. Order a shoebox full to go and be prepared to fight to keep your fellow passengers' hands off of 'em. They are really, really good!

15 Best Airport Restaurants

2,347 Runner-Ups

AKRON, OH

Arby's — *Fast Food*
Terminal 1

Great Lakes Brewing Co — *Coffee*
Terminal 1

Java Coast Coffee — *Coffee*
Terminal 1

JJ's Sports Bar — *Bar*
Main Terminal

Subway and Grill — *Deli*
Main Terminal

ALBANY, NY

Arrezzio's — *Italian*
Terminal A

Capital Deli and Pub — *Bar*
Terminal B

Checkpoint Cafe — *American*
Main Terminal 2nd Floor

Coffee Beanery — *Coffee*
Terminal C
Food Court

McDonald's — *Fast Food*
Food Court

Saranac Brew House — *Bar*
Food Court

Saranac Street Pub — *Bar*
Terminal A

Villa Fresh Italian Kitchen — *Italian*
Food Court

15 Best Airport Restaurants

ALBUQUERQUE, NM

Baskin Robbins — *Desserts*
Terminal A/B Connector Food Court

Black Mesa Coffee Company — *Coffee*
Main Terminal Pre-Security
Main Terminal Baggage
Terminal A Car Rental

Black Mesa Kiosk — *Mexican*
Terminal A — (505) 842-2417

Comida Buena Gourmet Deli — *Deli*
Terminal A/B Connector Food Court

Garduno's Chile Packing Co & Cantina — *Mexican*
Main Terminal Pre-Security

La Hacienda Mexican Restaurant — *Mexican*
Terminal A/B Connector Food Court — (505) 764-9129

Pizzeria Express — *Italian*
Terminal A/B Connector Food Court — (505) 884-7484

Puerto del Sol Lounge — *Bar*
Terminal B

Quizno's — *Deli*
Terminal A

Route 66 Microbrewery — *Bar*
Terminal A/B Connector Food Court — (505) 884-7484

Snack Bar — *Snacks*
Terminal B — (505) 884-7484

Winners Sports Bar — *Bar*
Terminal A — (505) 842-4079

ALLENTOWN, PA

LA Cafe — *American*
Ticket Area Gate

15 Best Airport Restaurants

Subway   *Deli*
    Ticket Area Gate

ANCHORAGE, AK

Burger King   *Fast Food*
    South Terminal Gate B3

Chili's Too   *American*
    South Terminal Gate C1

Cinnabon   *Desserts*
    South Terminal Gate B3

Cloud Hoppers Lounge   *Bar*
    South Terminal Gate B7

Cross Point Cafe   *American*
    North Terminal Gate N3

Cross Point Lounge   *Bar*
    North Terminal Gate N3

Host Food Court   *Fast Food*
    South Terminal Food Court

Legend's Lounge   *Bar*
    South Terminal Gate C6

Quizno's   *Deli*
    South Terminal Gate C3

Starbucks   *Coffee*
    South Terminal Gate C1
    South Terminal Lobby

Upper One Lounge   *American*
    South Terminal Lobby

ATLANTA, GA

Atlanta Bread Company   *Sandwiches*
    Atrium NE   404-768-2259

Au Bon Pain   *Deli*
    Terminal B Centerpoint   404-530-7514

15 Best Airport Restaurants

    Terminal D Gate 15   404-530-7535

Ben and Jerry's Ice Cream   *Desserts*
    Terminal A Gate 25   404-766-1902
    Terminal C Centerpoint   404-767-5086

Brews and Blues Bar   *Bar*
    Terminal T Gate 12   404-530-7538

Brews and Blues Bar & Hot Dog City   *American*
    Terminal A Gate 1   404-530-7543

Budweiser Brewhouse   *American*
    Terminal A Centerpoint   404-768-3448

Burger King   *Fast Food*
    Terminal A Gate 11   404-530-7542
    Terminal D Gate 7   404-530-7536
    Terminal D Gate 30   404-530-7541
    Terminal E Centerpoint   404-530-3662
    Terminal T Gate 9   404-530-7537

Charley's Steakery   *American*
    Terminal B Gate 13   404-305-9941
    Terminal C Gate 12   404-308-0187

Chick fil A   *Fast Food*
    Terminal A Gate 11   404-530-7542

Chili's Too   *American*
    Terminal A Centerpoint   404-530-7513

Cinnabon   *Bakery*
    Terminal A Gate 11   404-530-7542
    Terminal D Gate 7   404-530-7536
    Terminal D Gate 30   404-530-7541

Concorde Restro Bar   *Bar*
    Terminal E Gate 29   404-559-9429

Dominos Pizza   *Italian*
    Terminal A Centerpoint   404-766-0369
    Atrium SE   404-761-7316

Edy's Grand Ice Cream   *Desserts*
    Atrium SW   404-209-9007
    Terminal B Gate 9   404-762-0038

15 Best Airport Restaurants

Freshen   *Coffee*
    Terminal D Gate 16   404-530-2473

Great Wraps   *American*
    Terminal A Centerpoint   404-209-7506

Hartsfield Bistro   *Deli*
    Terminal T Gate 8   404-767-7112

Haussmann Restro Bar   *Bar*
    Terminal E Gate 9   404-559-3659

Hot Dog City   *Fast Food*
    Terminal E Centerpoint   404-766-4603

Hot Dog Construction Company   *Fast Food*
    Terminal A Centerpoint   404-765-0009

Houlihan's   *American*
    Terminal A Gate 25   404-762-1052
    Atrium Gate 2nd/3rd NE   404-761-4501

Krystal   *Fast Food*
    Terminal A Gate 28

Last Call South   *Bar*
    Terminal C Gate 6   404-768-3855

LePetit Bistro   *Deli*
    Terminal E Centerpoint   404-305-9808

Magnolia Bar and Grille   *American*
    Terminal B Gate 11   404-559-9787

Manchu Wok   *Chinese*
    Terminal A Centerpoint   404-209-0170
    Atrium SE   404-765-0888

Mandarin Express   *Oriental*
    Terminal B Centerpoint   404-305-8899
    Terminal E Centerpoint   404-305-8328

Miller Lite Victory Lane   *Bar*
    Terminal C Gate 9   404-761-2919

Nathan's Famous Hot Dogs   *Fast Food*
    Terminal B Gate 27   404-766-2444
    Terminal D Centerpoint   404-767-4224

15 Best Airport Restaurants

    Terminal T Gate 7   404-765-0450

Paschal's Southern Delights   ***Regional***
    Terminal C Centerpoint   404-209-8335
    Terminal A Centerpoint   404-209-1757
    Atrium SE   404-761-4160

Pizza Hut   ***Italian***
    Terminal E Centerpoint   404-766-4603

Plane Delicious   ***American***
    Terminal A Centerpoint   404-768-6162

Popeye's Chicken   ***Fast Food***
    Terminal B Centerpoint   404-763-1444
    Terminal C Gate 17   404-768-2799
    Terminal E Centerpoint   404-684-9450

Red Brick Tavern   ***Bar***
    Terminal T Gate 3   404-530-3686

Samuel Adam's   ***Bar***
    Terminal C Gate 30   404-761-0154

Sbarro Pizza   ***Italian***
    Terminal B Centerpoint   404-530-7516

Seattle's Best Coffee   ***Coffee***
    Terminal B Gate 3   404-768-8347
    Terminal Atrium NW   404-766-0296
    Terminal B Centerpoint   404-768-8307
    Terminal C Gate 16   404-768-0840
    Terminal C Gate 25   404-768-0850

Sojourner's   ***Bar***
    Terminal D Gate 9   404-766-2518

Spizzico   ***Italian***
    Terminal T Gate 3   404-530-7534

Sports Scene   ***American***
    Terminal B Gate 26   404-559-9833

Starbucks   ***Coffee***
    Terminal A Gate 2   404-530-3674
    Terminal B Gate 30   404-530-7545
    Terminal D Gate 27   404-530-7517
    Terminal E Centerpoint   404-530-3663

15 Best Airport Restaurants

    Terminal T Gate 11   404-530-7539
    Terminal T Gate 3   404-530-6109

TCBY   *Desserts*
    Terminal A Gate 9   404-761-4742
    Terminal B Gate 23   404-765-0080
    Terminal D Gate 7   404-530-2473
    Terminal T Gate 3   404-767-6101

TGI Fridays   *American*
    Terminal B Centerpoint   404-763-3420

The Grove Natural Snacks   *Snacks*
    Terminal A Gate 12   404-530-2471
    Terminal C Centerpoint   404-530-2470

Vending Machines   *Snacks*
    Terminal A Gate 33   404-761-3312
    Terminal B Gate 2   404-761-3312
    Terminal B Gate 21   404-761-3312
    Terminal B Gate 28   404-761-3312
    Terminal C Gate 24   404-761-3312
    Terminal C Gate 31   404-761-3312
    Terminal C Gate 8   404-761-3312
    Terminal D Gate 14   404-761-3312
    Terminal D Gate 26   404-761-3312
    Terminal E Gate 17   404-761-3312
    Terminal E Gate 28   404-761-3312
    Terminal E Gate 8   404-761-3312

Wall Street Deli   *Deli*
    Terminal A Centerpoint   404-305-0615

Wendy's   *Fast Food*
    Atrium SE   404-761-2626
    Terminal C Gate 25   404-761-3122

AUSTIN, TX

Amy's Ice Creams   *Desserts*
    West Food Court

Auntie Anne's   *Snacks*
    East Food Court

Austin Java   *Coffee*
    Central Concourse

15 Best Airport Restaurants

Earl Campbell's Sports Bar — Bar
    West Concourse

Fara Cafe Sports Bar — Bar
    Ticket lobby

Harlon's Barbeque Bar and Grill — American
    East Concourse

Harlon's Country Breakfast and Barbecue — American
    East Food Court

Harlon's Espresso and News — Coffee
    Terminal West Entrance

Highland Lakes Bar — American
    Central Marketplace

Lefty's Bar and Grille on 6th Street — American
    West Concourse — (512) 530-2999

Mangia Pizza — Italian
    West Food Court

Schlotzsky's Deli — Deli
    West Food Court

The Salt Lick — American
    West Food Court

Waterloo Ice House — American
    East Food Court

Wok and Roll — Oriental
    East Food Court

BALTIMORE, MD

Arby's — Fast Food
    Terminal A/B Food Court

Au Bon Pain — Fast Food
    Terminal A/B Food Court

Auntie Anne's — Snacks
    Terminal A Gate 7

15 Best Airport Restaurants

    Terminal B Gate 1
    Terminal D Gate Food Court

Baci Bar and Grill   *Bar*
    Terminal A/B Landside Ticket

Beer Garden   *Bar*
    Terminal C Gate 8

Bill Bateman's Bistro   *Bar*
    Main Terminal Food Court

California Tortilla   *Mexican*
    Terminal A/B Food Court

Charlie Chang's KWAI   *Oriental*
    Terminal A/B Food Court

Chesapeake Bay Roasting Company   *Snacks*
    Terminal D

Godiva Chocolatier   *Desserts*
    Terminal A/B Food Court

Green Turtle Cafe   *American*
    Terminal D Gate 8

Hudson New Euro Cafe   *Coffee*
    Terminal A/B Baggage

Java City   *Coffee*
    Terminal A/B Food Court

Mamma Ilardo's Pizzeria   *Italian*
    Terminal A/B Food Court

Manchu Wok   *Oriental*
    Terminal D Food Court

Mayorga Coffee   *Coffee*
    Terminal A/B Food Court

McDonald's   *Fast Food*
    Terminal A/B Food Court
    Terminal D Food Court

Nature's Table Cafe   *Deli*
    Main Terminal Food Court

15 Best Airport Restaurants

Obrycki's Restaurant and Bar
Terminal B Gate 9
Seafood

Panda Express
Terminal B Food Court
Oriental

Phillip's Famous Seafood
Terminal A/B Food Court
Seafood

Potbelly Sandwich Works
Terminal C Food Court
Deli

Quizno's
Terminal A/B Food Court
Terminal D Food Court
Deli

Rum Island Bar
Terminal D Gate 22
Bar

Samuel Adams Brewhouse
Terminal E Gate 1
Bar

Shannon's Pub
Terminal D Gate 12
Bar

Silver Diner
Terminal A/B Food Court
American

Starbucks
Terminal B Gate 6
Main Terminal - Ticketing
Coffee

Subway
Terminal B Gate 3
Deli

Villa Pizza
Terminal A Food Court
Italian

Villa Pronto
Terminal B Gate 3
Italian

Villa Volla Wine Bar
Terminal A Gate 6
Bar

Wendy's
Terminal C Food Court
Fast Food

15 Best Airport Restaurants

Zona Mexicana — *Mexican*
Terminal B Gate 4

BIRMINGHAM, AL

Autographs Lounge — *Bar*
Terminal C

Charley's Steakery — *American*
Food Court

Freshens — *Healthy*
Terminal C

Golden Rule Barbeque — *Regional*
Food Court

Mrs. Field's Cookies — *Desserts*
Food Court

Pizza Hut Express — *Italian*
Food Court

Rotunda Snack Bar — *Healthy*
Terminal C

TCBY — *Desserts*
Food Court

Wall Street Deli — *Deli*
Terminal C

BOISE, ID

Concourse Bar — *Bar*
Food Court

Freshens — *Healthy*
Terminal B

Maui Taco — *Mexican*
Food Court

McDonald's — *American*
Food Court

15 Best Airport Restaurants

Moxie Java   *Coffee*
    Terminal C

Outpost Cafe   *American*
    Main Gate 2nd Floor

Varsity Grill and Sports Bar   *Bar*
    Terminal B

Villa Pizza   *Italian*
    Food Court

BOSTON, MA

Au Bon Pain   *Deli*
    Terminal A Gate 7   (617) 561-6020
    Terminal B
    Terminal C   (617) 567-4139
    Terminal E
    Terminal B

Bella Boston   *Italian*
    Terminal B

Boston Cafe   *Deli*
    Terminal B

Burger King   *Fast Food*
    Terminal C   (617) 634-6064

Burger King Expressway   *Fast Food*
    Terminal B
    Terminal C

Caffe Ritazza   *Italian*
    Terminal B

Cibo Express   *Deli*
    Terminal C Gate 29

Dine Boston Bar and Grill   *American*
    Terminal E

Dunkin Donuts   *Desserts*
    Terminal A Gate 8   (617) 569-4364
    Terminal A Gate 17   (617) 569-4364
    Terminal B Gate 30

15 Best Airport Restaurants

Terminal C
Terminal E
Terminal C

Famous Famiglia *Italian*
    Terminal A Food Court   (617) 561-8517

FOX Sports Sky Box Bar and Grill *Bar*
    Terminal B

Fresh City *Deli*
    Terminal A Food Court   (617) 561-0447

Fuddrucker's *Fast Food*
    Terminal A Food Court   (617) 5671330

Game On *Bar*
    Terminal A Food Court   (617) 567-0292

Gourmet on the Fly *Snacks*
    Terminal A Gate 20
    Terminal C Gate 20

Grab and Go Cafe *Deli*
    Terminal B Gate 37

Greenleaf's Grille *Deli*
    Terminal C

Houlihan's *American*
    Terminal E

Jasper White's Summer Shack *American*
    Terminal A Gate 13   (617) 569-9695

Java Coast *Coffee*
    Terminal E

Johnny Rocket's *American*
    Terminal C

Killian's Boston Pub *Bar*
    Terminal B

Legal Sea Foods Cafe *American*
    Terminal B
    Terminal C
    Terminal A Gate 2   (617) 568-1888

15 Best Airport Restaurants

Lucky's
    Terminal A Gate 6

Italian
(617) 567-0292

McDonald's
    Terminal E

Fast Food

Ozone Bos
    Terminal B

Bar

Pizza Hut Express
    Terminal B

Italian

Pizzeria Uno
    Terminal C

Italian

Samuel Adam's
    Terminal C Gate 25

Bar

Sbarro
    Terminal B
    Terminal E

Italian

Starbucks
    Terminal A Food Court
    Terminal B
    Terminal C
    Terminal E

Coffee
(617) 634-6006

The Grove
    Terminal C

Snacks
(617) 561-0328

Wendy's
    Terminal A Gate 8

Fast Food

Wok and Roll
    Terminal E

Oriental

Wolfgang Puck
    Terminal B
    Terminal C Gate 25

American

BUFFALO, NY

AllStar's Bar
    Lobby Post Security

Bar

15 Best Airport Restaurants

Burger King — *Fast Food*
  Lobby Pre Security

Cinnabon — *Desserts*
  Lobby Pre Security

Freshens — *Snacks*
  Gate 4

Jake's Bistro and News — *Deli*
  Gate 21

Landmark Bar and Carvery — *American*
  Gate 9

Mattie's Texas Red Hots — *American*
  Gate 21
  Gate 4

Niagara Grill — *American*
  Lobby Pre Security

The Coffee Beanery — *Coffee*
  Lobby Post Security

Wings to Go — *American*
  Gate 9 — (877) 946-478

CEDAR RAPIDS, IA

Blue Strawberry Coffee Co — *Coffee*
  Terminal A

Creative Croissants — *Fast Food*
  Terminal A

Sam Adams — *Bar*
  Terminal A

CHARLOTTE, NC

Brookwood Farms BBQ — *American*
  Atrium

Budweiser Brewhouse — *Bar*
  Terminal D

15 Best Airport Restaurants

Burger King   *Fast Food*
   Atrium

California Pizza Kitchen   *American*
   Terminal B

California Pizza Kitchen To Go   *American*
   Terminal B

Caribbean Marketplace   *Fast Food*
   Terminal D

Carolina Sports Bar   *Bar*
   Terminal C

Charlotte Bistro   *Deli*
   Baggage

Chili's   *American*
   Atrium

Chili's To Go   *American*
   Atrium

Cinnabon   *Desserts*
   Terminal A
   Terminal E
   Atrium

Coca Cola 600 Cafe   *American*
   Terminal D

Edy's Ice Cream   *Desserts*
   Terminal E

First In Flight Bar   *Bar*
   Atrium

Fox Skybox   *Deli*
   Terminal E

Frankly Gourmet   *American*
   Terminal Atrium

Freschetta Pizza   *Italian*
   Terminal D

Fresh Attractions   *Deli*

15 Best Airport Restaurants

    Terminal C

Fresh Attractions Kiosk   *Snacks*
    Terminal E

Freshens Frozen Treats   *Desserts*
    Terminal B
    Terminal Atrium

Great American Bagel   *Deli*
    Terminal B
    Terminal D

Jamba Juice   *Snacks*
    Terminal D/E Connector

Jose Cuervo Tequileria   *Bar*
    Terminal Atrium

KFC Express   *Fast Food*
    Terminal A

Manchu Wok   *Oriental*
    Terminal Atrium

Mrs. Field's Cookies   *Desserts*
    Terminal Atrium

Nathan's   *Fast Food*
    Terminal C

Phillips Famous Seafood   *American*
    Terminal C

Pino Gelato   *Desserts*
    Terminal B

Pizza Hut   *Italian*
    Terminal Atrium

Quiznos   *Deli*
    Terminal Atrium

Ranch 1   *Fast Food*
    Terminal B

Sbarro   *Italian*
    Terminal C

15 Best Airport Restaurants

Snack-N-Run   *Snacks*
    Terminal A

Speedway Grill   *American*
    Terminal E

Starbucks   *Coffee*
    Terminal B
    Terminal C
    Terminal Ticketing
    Terminal D/E Connector
    Terminal Atrium

Stock Car Cafe   *American*
    Terminal B

Taste of Carolina Bar   *Bar*
    Terminal B

TCBY   *Desserts*
    Terminal C

Wolfgang Puck   *American*
    Terminal E

World Traveler Bar   *Bar*
    Terminal A

Yadkin Valley Wine Bar   *Bar*
    Terminal D/E Connector

Yovana Yogurt Cafe   *Snacks*
    Terminal Atrium

CHICAGO (Midway), IL

Ben and Jerry's   *Desserts*
    Triangle

Dot Com Cafe   *American*
    Terminal A

EuroCafe   *Deli*
    Triangle

Gold Coast Dogs   *Fast Food*

15 Best Airport Restaurants

    Triangle

Halsted Tap   *Bar*
    Terminal A

Harry Caray's 7TH Inning Stretch   *American*
    Triangle   773.948.6300

Illinois Bar and Grill   *American*
    Triangle

King Wah Express   *Oriental*
    Triangle

Lalo's Mexican Restaurant   *Mexican*
    Triangle

Let Them Eat Cake   *Desserts*
    Terminal B

Manny's Deli   *Deli*
    Terminal A

McDonald's   *Fast Food*
    Terminal A

Miller's Pub   *Bar*
    Terminal B

Nuts on Clark   *Snacks*
    Terminal B

Oak Street Beach Cafe   *American*
    Terminal B

Potbelly Sandwich Works   *Deli*
    Triangle

Reillys Daughter   *Deli*
    Triangle

Southside Pizzeria   *Italian*
    Terminal B

Superdawg   *Fast Food*
    Terminal B

Taylor Street Market   *Deli*

Terminal B

Tuscany *Italian*
   Terminal A

CHICAGO (O'Hare), IL

Artist and Writer *Bar*
   Terminal 1

Berghoff Cafe *Deli*
   Terminal 1

Billy Goat Tavern and Grill *Fast Food*
   Terminal 1

Budweiser Bar *Bar*
   Terminal 1

Burrito Beach B Smooth *Mexican*
   Terminal 3

Cafe Zoot *American*
   Terminal 1

Chicago Bar and Grill *Bar*
   Terminal 3

Chicago Style Hot Dogs *Fast Food*
   Terminal 1

Chili's *American*
   Terminal 3
   Terminal 1
   Terminal 2

Cinnabon *Desserts*
   Terminal 1
   Terminal 2
   Terminal 3

Connie's Pizza *Italian*
   Terminal 1

Corner Bakery *Deli*
   Terminal 1
   Terminal 3

15 Best Airport Restaurants

Deli Bar *Deli*
    Terminal 3

Dunkin Donuts *Desserts*
    Terminal 3

Elis Cheesecake *Desserts*
    Terminal 1

Facades Bar *Bar*
    Terminal 3

Fox Sports Sky Box *Bar*
    Terminal 2 (773) 686-6105
    Terminal 3 (773) 686-6105

Galileo's *Bar*
    Terminal 1

Gold Coast Dogs *Fast Food*
    Terminal 3
    Terminal 5

Goose Island Brewing Company *Bar*
    Terminal 2

Great American Bagel *Deli*
    Terminal 1
    Terminal 3

Haagen Dazs *Desserts*
    Terminal 5

Hixon's Popcorn *Snacks*
    Terminal 1

Jazz Bar *Bar*
    Terminal 1

Juicework's *Deli*
    Terminal 2
    Terminal 3

Lou Mitchells Express *Deli*
    Terminal 5

Manchu Wok *Oriental*

15 Best Airport Restaurants

    Terminal 1
    Terminal 3

McDonald's   *Fast Food*
    Terminal 1
    Terminal 2
    Terminal 3
    Terminal 5

Mrs. Field's Cookies   *Desserts*
    Terminal 3

O'Brien's Restaurant   *American*
    Terminal 3

Parades Bar   *Bar*
    Terminal 5

Pizzeria Uno   *Italian*
    Terminal 2
    Terminal 3
    Terminal 5

Prairie Tap   *Bar*
    Terminal 3

Quick Connection   *Deli*
    Terminal 1
    Terminal 2

Quizno's   *Fast Food*
    Terminal 1
    Terminal 2

Reggio's Pizza   *Italian*
    Terminal 1
    Terminal 3

Salad Works   *Deli*
    Terminal 1

Sky Bridge Restaurant   *Deli*
    Terminal 2

Starbucks   *Coffee*
    Terminal 1
    Terminal 2
    Terminal 3

15 Best Airport Restaurants

TCBY — *Desserts*
    Terminal 1 — 773-686-8473
    Terminal 2 — 773-686-8473
    Terminal 3 — 773-686-8473

The Grove — *Snacks*
    Terminal 1
    Terminal 2

The Meridian Bar — *Bar*
    Terminal 3

Waterworks — *Deli*
    Terminal 3

Windy City Yogurt — *Desserts*
    Terminal 5

Wolfgang Puck — *American*
    Terminal 1
    Terminal 3

CLEVELAND, OH

Ben and Jerry's Ice Cream — *Desserts*
    Terminal C

Burger King — *Fast Food*
    Terminal B

Cafe Connection — *American*
    Terminal C

Cafe Connection Express — *Deli*
    Terminal A

Cinnabon — *Desserts*
    Terminal A
    Terminal B
    Terminal C

Cleveland Brews — *Bar*
    Terminal C

Cleveland Fruit and Nut — *Snacks*
    Terminal C

15 Best Airport Restaurants

Fresh Attractions *Deli*
    Terminal A

Great American Bagel   *Deli*
    Terminal C
    Terminal D

Great Lakes Brewing Company   *American*
    Terminal A

Home Turf Sports Bar   *Bar*
    Terminal D

Jody Maroni   *American*
    Terminal D

Manchu Wok   *Oriental*
    Terminal B

Max and Erma's   *American*
    Terminal B
    Terminal C

Nathan's   *Fast Food*
    Terminal A
    Terminal B

Onstage Cafe   *American*
    Terminal C

Pierre's Ice Cream   *Desserts*
    Terminal B

Pizza Hut   *Italian*
    Terminal A
    Terminal D

PSAir Pub   *Bar*
    Terminal A

Sbarro   *Fast Food*
    Terminal C

Starbucks   *Coffee*
    Terminal C
    Terminal D
    Ticketing

15 Best Airport Restaurants

Ticketing

TCBY *Desserts*
    Terminal B
    Terminal C
    Terminal D

Tequileria — *Mexican*
    Terminal C

Westside Market Deli — *Deli*
    Terminal B

COLORADO SPRINGS, CO

A&W — *Fast Food*
    Main Terminal 2nd Floor

Cantina Azul — *Mexican*
    Main Terminal FC

Freshen — *Healthy*
    Main Terminal 2nd Floor

Gordon Biersch — *American*
    Main Terminal 2nd Floor

Pikes Perk — *Coffee*
    Main Terminal 2nd Floor
    Main Terminal FC

Pizza Hut Express — *Italian*
    Main Terminal FC

Quizno's — *Deli*
    Main Terminal FC

COLUMBUS, OH

Arrivederci Bar — *Bar*
    Terminal Concourse B

Buckeye Hall of Fame Cafe — *American*
    Terminal Concourse B

Ciao Gourmet Market — *Deli*

15 Best Airport Restaurants

Terminal Concourse B

Columbus Brewing Company   *Bar*
Terminal Concourse B Gate 21

Quizno's   *Deli*
Terminal Concourse B

Starbucks   *Coffee*
Terminal Concourse B

Wolfgang Puck   *American*
Terminal Concourse A
Terminal Concourse B

CORPUS CHRISTI, TX

Game Time Sports Restaurant and Lounge   *Bar*
Main Gate Lobby

Hangtime   *Fast Food*
Main Gate Area

Le Paris Cafe   *Deli*
Main Gate Lobby

Windy City Eatery   *American*
Main Gate Lobby

COVINGTON, KY

360 Gourmet Burrito   *Mexican*
Terminal B Gate 21   (859)767-5798

Auntie Anne's *Snacks*
Terminal C Gate 20   (859)767-1940

Bluegrass Brewing Co   *American*
Terminal C Gate 79   (859)767-1067

Bridgeworks Deli   *Deli*
Ticketing Gate 3   (859)767-1063

Carvel   *Desserts*
Terminal B Food Court

15 Best Airport Restaurants

Chick fil A   *Fast food*
    Terminal B Food Court   (859)767-1076

Cinnabon   *Desserts*
    Terminal B Food Court

Damon's Grill   *American*
    Terminal 2 Ticketing   (859)767-1982

Dunkin Donut's   *Desserts*
Terminal C Gate Center Lobby

Gas Light Baking Co   *Deli*
    Terminal 2 Gate Ticketing   (859)767-6078
    Terminal C Gate 40   (859)767-5714

Gold Star Chili   *Fast Food*
    Terminal B Gate Food Court   (859)767-5612

Great Steak and Potato   *Fast Food*
    Terminal B Gate Food Court

Grove   *Snacks*
    Terminal A Gate 14   (859)767-3793
    Terminal B Gate Center Hub   (859)767-7878
    Terminal C Gate 60   (859)767-5893
    Terminal B Gate 17
    Terminal C Gate 19   (859)767-3638

Ida's Seat   *American*
    Terminal B Gate 26   (859)767-5552

Max and Erma's   *American*
Terminal B Gate 9   (859)767-1985

McDonald's   *Fast Food*
    Terminal B Food Court   (859)767-3295
    Terminal C Center lobby   (859)767-3294

Moe's Grill and Bar   *American*
    Terminal A Gate 14   (859)767-6085
    Terminal C Center Lobby   (859)767-5584

Mrs. Field's Cookies   *Desserts*
    Terminal B Food Court   (859)767-1070

Outback Steakhouse   *American*
    Terminal B Center Hub   (859)767-1055

15 Best Airport Restaurants

Panda Express
    Terminal A Gate 12

Oriental
(859)767-5787

Peet's Coffee and Tea
    Terminal A Gate 2
    Terminal B Gate 8

Coffee
(859)767-3720
(859)767-1987

Qdoba Mexican Grill
    Terminal C Gate 30

Mexican
(859)767-5977

Queen City Popcorn
    Terminal B Gate Center Hub

Snacks
(859)767-5856

Quizno's
    Terminal A Gate 11

Fast Food
(859)767-5856

Samuel Adams Celebrates Cincinnati
    Terminal A Gate 16

Bar
(859)767-1242

Sbarro
    Terminal B Food Court

Fast Food
(859)767-1059

Starbucks
    Terminal B Center Hub
    Terminal C Center Lobby
    Terminal 3 Ticketing

Coffee
(859)767-1054
(859)767-6020
(859)767-1063

Subway
    Terminal C Gate 30

Fast Food
(859)767-6046

TCBY
    Terminal B Food Court

Desserts
(859)767-1070

The Pub
    Terminal C Gate 1

Deli
(859)767-5776

Wetzel's Pretzels
    Terminal B Gate 19
    Terminal 2 Gate Ticketing

Snacks
(859)767-5973
(859)767-5580

Wolfgang Puck
    Terminal B Gate 17

American
(859)767-4970

DALLAS-FORT WORTH, TX
Au Bon Pain   *Deli*

15 Best Airport Restaurants

    Terminal A Gate 13
    Terminal A Gate 25
    Terminal A Gate 38
    Terminal B Gate 20
    Terminal C Gate 24
    Terminal C Gate 31
    Terminal D Gate 28

Auntie Anne's Pretzels — *Snacks*
    Terminal A Gate 25
    Terminal A Gate 39
    Terminal B Gate 6
    Terminal C Gate 24
    Terminal D Gate 12
    Terminal E Gate 15

Ben and Jerry's — *Desserts*
    Terminal D Gate 12
    Terminal D Gate 27

Bennigan's Grill and Tavern — *American*
    Terminal D Gate 11

Blue Bamboo Xpress — *Oriental*
    Terminal D Gate 31

Blue Mesa Taco and Tequila Bar — *Mexican*
    Terminal D Gate 31

Burger King — *Fast Food*
    Terminal E Gate 5

Camille's Sidewalk Cafe — *Deli*
    Terminal D Gate 27

Candy Headquarters — *Snacks*
    Terminal A Gate 22

Cantina Laredo — *Mexican*
    Terminal D Gate 27

Champ's Grill and Bar — *American*
    Terminal D Gate 24

Chili's Too — *American*
    Terminal B Gate 19
    Terminal C Gate 15

15 Best Airport Restaurants

Cool River Cafe *American*
    Terminal D Gate 25

Cousins BBQ *American*
    Terminal D Gate 28

Cowtown Bar *Bar*
    Terminal A Gate 35

Dickey's BBQ *American*
    Terminal A Gate 18
    Terminal C Gate 6
    Terminal E Gate 12

East Side Mario's *Italian*
    Terminal A Gate 38

Einstein Bros Bagels *Deli*
    Terminal D Gate 18

Freshen's *Desserts*
    Terminal B Gate 8
    Terminal B Gate 8
    Terminal C Gate 6
    Terminal E Gate 5

Friday's America Bar *American*
    Terminal B Gate 12
    Terminal C Gate 8
    Terminal C Gate 30

Frullati Cafe and Bakery *Italian*
    Terminal A Gate 9
    Terminal A Gate 9
    Terminal B Gate 8
    Terminal C Gate 6
    Terminal C Gate 24

Fuddrucker's *Fast Food*
    Terminal D Gate 18
    Terminal D Gate 18

Haagen Daz s *Desserts*
    Terminal E Gate 15
    Terminal C Gate 17

Harlon's BBQ Grill and Bar *American*
    Terminal B Gate 25
    Terminal B Gate 34

15 Best Airport Restaurants

Hebrew National   *Fast Food*
    Terminal A Gate 25

Hot Dog Construction Company   *Fast Food*
    Terminal B Gate 15

I Can't Believe Its Yogurt   *Desserts*
    Terminal A Gate 13
    Terminal A Gate 25
    Terminal A Gate 39
    Terminal C Gate 24

Jazzman's Cafe   *Coffee*
    Terminal D Gate 28
    Terminal D Gate 10
    Terminal D Gate 10

La Bodega Winery and Tasting Bar   *Bar*
    Terminal D Gate 14
    Terminal A Gate 15

Los Amigos Tex Mex   *Mexican*
    Terminal A Gate 37

Manchu Wok   *Oriental*
    Terminal C Gate 24
    Terminal C Gate 24
    Terminal E Gate 15
    Terminal A Gate 25

McDonald's   *Fast Food*
    Terminal A Gate 25
    Terminal A Gate 13
    Terminal B Gate 29
    Terminal C Gate 24
    Terminal C Gate 6
    Terminal D Gate 33

Mr Gatti's Pizza   *Italian*
    Terminal E Gate 15

Pizza Hut Express   *Italian*
    Terminal B Gate 10
    Terminal C Gate 6
    Terminal C Gate 20
    Terminal C Gate 31

15 Best Airport Restaurants

Popeye's Chicken and Biscuits *Fast Food*
    Terminal A Gate 13
    Terminal D Gate 22

Reata Grill *American*
    Terminal D Gate 33

Rider's World Bar *Bar*
    Terminal E Gate 15

Sbarros Italian Eatery *Italian*
    Terminal B Gate 4

Seattle's Best Coffee *Coffee*
    Terminal A Gate 14
    Terminal B Gate 8
    Terminal C Gate 6
    Terminal C Gate 21
    Terminal E Gate 5

Starbucks *Coffee*
    Terminal A Gate 13
    Terminal A Gate 29
    Terminal A Gate 33
    Terminal B Gate 28
    Terminal B Gate 14
    Terminal C Gate 12
    Terminal C Gate 27
    Terminal D Gate 25
    Terminal E Gate 8

Subway *Fast Food*
    Terminal A Gate 33

Taco Bell Express *Mexican*
    Terminal A Gate 13
    Terminal C Gate 14
    Terminal E Gate 15
    Terminal E Gate 5

Texas Stadium Skybox *Bar*
    Terminal A Gate 10
    Terminal B Gate 6

TGI Friday's *American*
    Terminal A Gate 22
    Terminal D Gate 34
    Terminal E Gate 17

15 Best Airport Restaurants

The Grove   *Snacks*
    Terminal A Gate 17
    Terminal A Gate 39
    Terminal E Gate 7

Tigin Irish Pub and Restaurant   *Bar*
    Terminal D Gate 20

Vintage Texas   *American*
    Terminal A Gate 16
    Terminal E Gate 12

Wendy's   *Fast Food*
    Terminal C Gate 14

DALLAS (LOVE), TX

Antler's Bar   *Bar*
    Terminal 2 Gate 4

Chili's Bar and Bites   *American*
    Terminal 2 Main Lobby

Chili's Too   *American*
    Terminal 2 Gate 2

Dreyer's Ice Cream   *Desserts*
    Terminal 2 Gate 4

Gate 9 Bar   *Bar*
    Terminal 2 Gate 9

Hot Dog Construction Company   *Fast Food*
    Terminal 2 Gate 9
    Terminal 2 Gate 4

McDonald's   *Fast Food*
    Terminal 2 Gate 4

Oasis Bakery and Deli   *Deli*
    Terminal 2 Gate 4
    Terminal 2 Gate 9
    Terminal 2 Gate 27

Pizza Hut Express   *Italian*
    Terminal 2 Gate 4

15 Best Airport Restaurants

Terminal 2 Gate 9

Seattle's Best Coffee   *Coffee*
Terminal 2 Gate 6

DAYTON, OH

Boston Stoker   *Coffee*
Terminal Main Gate FC

Cinnabon   *Bakery*
Terminal Main Gate FC

Dayton's All Stars Cafe   *Bar*
Terminal Main Gate FC

Max and Erma's   *American*
Terminal Main Gate FC

Sbarro's   *Deli*
Terminal Main Gate FC

The Tool Town Tavern   *Bar*
Terminal Main Gate FC

DENVER, CO

Air Meals   *Deli*
Terminal C   303-342-3427
Auntie Anne's Pretzels   *Snacks*
Terminal B   303-342-3359
Main Terminal   303-342-8450

Aviator's Club Smoking Lounge   *Bar*
Main Terminal   303-342-7577

Brew Mountain Express   *Coffee*
Main Terminal   303-342-8446

Burger King   *Fast Food*
Main Terminal   303-342-8444

Cantina Grill Express   *Mexican*
Main Terminal   303-342-6872

Cantina Grill Express   *Mexican*

15 Best Airport Restaurants

Terminal A	303-342-3410
Terminal B	303-342-6860
Terminal C	303-342-6867

Chef Jimmy's Bistro and Spirits — *Bar*
Terminal A — 303-342-5882

Cinnabites — *Desserts*
Terminal B — 303-342-7594

Colombo Frozen Yogurt *Desserts*
Terminal B — 303-342-0158
Terminal B — 303-342-3372

Colorado Sports Bar and Deli — *Bar*
Terminal B — 303-342-6831

CowBoy Bar — *Bar*
Terminal A — 303-342-3377

Creative Croissants — *Deli*
Main Terminal — 303-342-3570

Denver's Picture Show Popcorn — *Snacks*
Terminal A — 303-342-3466

Dominos Pizza — *Italian*
Main Terminal — 303-342-3395
Terminal A — 303-342-3397

Hixson's Popcorn — *Snacks*
Terminal B — 303-342-8589

Hope's Country Fresh Cookies — *Desserts*
Terminal A — 303-342-0300

Itza Wrap Itza Bowl — *Deli*
Terminal B — 303-317-0991

Kentucky Fired Chicken — *Fast Food*
Terminal A — 303-342-9044

Lefty's Colorado Trails Bar and Grille — *American*
Terminal A — 303-342-7177

Lefty's Front Range Grille — *American*
Terminal C — 303-342-7179

15 Best Airport Restaurants

Lefty's Mile High Grille   *American*
    Terminal B   303-342-7178

McDonald's   *Fast Food*
    Terminal A   303-342-9048
    Terminal B   303-342-9050
    Terminal C   303-342-9052

Noble Roman Pizza *Italian*
    Terminal B   303-342-0158

Panda Express   *Chinese*
    Main Terminal   303-342-3403
    Terminal A   303-342-3405

Pizza Hut Express   *Italian*
    Terminal A   303-342-9044

Pour La France Cafe and Bar   *Bar*
    Main Terminal   303-317-9470
    Terminal B   303-317-9472

Que Bueno Mexican Grille   *Mexican*
    Terminal B   303-342-3372

Quizno's Classic Subs and Bar   *Fast Food*
    Terminal A   303-342-7363
    Terminal B   303-342-0697

Red Rocks Bar   *Bar*
    Main Terminal   303-342-7176

Rocky Mountain Chocolate Factory   *Desserts*
    Terminal B East   303-342-3472
    Terminal B West   303-342-7860

Sara Lee Sandwich   *Deli*
    Terminal B   303-342-3372

Seattle's Best Coffee   *Coffee*
    Main Terminal   303-342-3416
    Terminal B   303-342-3419

SkySnax   *Snacks*
    Terminal B   303-342-3451
    Terminal C   303-342-3452

Steak Escape   *American*

15 Best Airport Restaurants

Terminal B — 303-342-3445

Stephany's Chocolates — *Desserts*
Main Terminal — 303-342-0735

Taco Bell — *Mexican*
Main Terminal — 303-342-5547

TCBY Yogurt and Ice Cream — *Desserts*
Main Terminal — 303-342-3400
Terminal B — 303-342-3401
Terminal C — 303-342-3402

Villa Italian Specialities — *Italian*
Terminal C — 303-342-0256

Wolfgang Puck — *American*
Terminal B — 303-317-9474

DES MOINES, IA

American Grill — *American*
Main Terminal FC

Capital City Brew Pub — *Bar*
Main Terminal FC

Creative Croissants — *Deli*
Lobby FC

Friedrich's Coffee Shop — *Coffee*
Lobby FC

Pizzeria Uno — *Italian*
Lobby FC

Sports Bar — *Bar*
Lobby FC

DETROIT, MI

American Coney Island — *Fast Food*
Terminal Smith Gate C

A&W — *Fast Food*
Terminal McNamara Gate B5 — (734) 955-7055

15 Best Airport Restaurants

BB Kings Bar and Grill — *American*
Terminal Smith Gate C

Bricktown — *Bar*
Terminal Smith Gate A

Burger King — *Fast Food*
Terminal McNamara — (734) 857-1300

Caribou Coffee — *Coffee*
Terminal McNamara Gate A60

Caribou Coffee — *Coffee*
Terminal McNamara Gate A74

Charley's Grilled Subs — *American*
Terminal McNamara Gate A74 — (734) 955-7055

Chili's — *American*
Terminal McNamara Gate A36 — (734) 857-1300
Terminal Smith Gate C

Coffee Beanery — *Coffee*
Terminal McNamara Gate A10
Terminal McNamara Gate B18 — (734) 229-0616
Terminal McNamara Gate C11 — (734) 229-0616

Detroit 500 — *Bar*
Terminal McNamara Gate C31

Detroit to Go — *Fast Food*
Terminal Smith Gate A11

Diego's Mexican Cantina — *Mexican*
Terminal McNamara Gate A12 — (734) 955-7055

Edy's Ice Cream — *Desserts*
Terminal McNamara Gate A74

Einstein Bros. Bagels — *Deli*
Terminal McNamara Gate B2

Food Buffet — *American*
Terminal Berry Gate

Fox Skybox — *Bar*
Terminal McNamara Central — (734) 857-1300

15 Best Airport Restaurants

Fresh Attractions — *Snacks*
    Terminal Snacks Gate A
    Terminal Smith Gate B
    Terminal Smith Gate C
    Terminal Berry Ticketing

Fuddrucker's — *Fast Food* (734) 247-6887
    Terminal McNamara Gate C25

Grey Goose Martini Lounge — *Bar* (734) 247-6887
    Terminal McNamara Gate C19

Hungry Howie's Pizza — *Italian* (734) 229-0616
    Terminal McNamara Gate A1

Java Coast CafÃ© — *Coffee* (734) 955-7055
    Terminal McNamara Intl Arrivals

Jose Cuervo Tequileria — *Bar* (734) 857-1300
    Terminal McNamara Gate A66
    Terminal Smith Center

Little Caesars Pizza — *Italian* (734) 857-1300
    Terminal McNamara Central

Lounge — *Bar*
    Terminal Berry

Max and Erma's — *American*
    Terminal McNamara Gate A30

McDonald's — *Fast Food* (734) 247-4366
    Terminal McNamara Gate A36

Mediterranean Grill — *Deli* (734) 941-9330
    Terminal McNamara Gate A54

Mrs. Field's Cookies — *Desserts* (734) 229-0616
    Terminal McNamara Gate A1

Musashi — *Oriental* (734) 247-6785
    Terminal McNamara Gate Central

National Coney Island — *Fast Food* (734) 955-1733
    Terminal McNamara Gate A46
    Terminal Smith Center

15 Best Airport Restaurants

National Coney Island Express *Fast Food*
    Terminal McNamara Gate A24   (734) 955-1733

Online Cafe *American*
    Terminal McNamara Gate A36   (734) 942-9791

PB and J   *Deli*
    Terminal McNamara Gate A1   (734) 229-0616

PizzaPapalis   *Italian*
    Terminal McNamara Gate A60   (734) 955-7055

Pizzeria Uno   *Italian*
    Terminal Smith Gate C

Quizno's   *Deli*
    Terminal McNamara Gate A1   (734) 229-0616
    Terminal Smith Gate A
    Terminal Smith Gate B

Rio Wraps   *Deli*
    Terminal McNamara Gate A60   (734) 955-7055

Rival's   *Bar*
    Terminal Smith Gate B

SlapShotz   *Bar*
    Terminal McNamara Gate A24   (734) 955-2003

Sora Japanese Cuisine and Sushi Bar   *Oriental*
    Terminal McNamara Gate A35   (734) 229-0209

Starbucks   *Coffee*
    Terminal McNamara Central   (734) 857-1300
    Terminal McNamara Gate A40   (734) 857-1300
    Terminal Smith Center
    Terminal Smith Gate A
    Terminal Smith Gate B
    Terminal Smith Baggage

Taco Bell   *Fast Food*
    Terminal McNamara Gate A74   (734) 955-7055

Tailpipe Tap   *Bar*
    Terminal McNamara Gate A74   (734) 955-7055

TCBY   *Desserts*
    Terminal McNamara Central   (734) 857-1300

15 Best Airport Restaurants

Thee Irish/Guinness Pub — *Bar* — (734) 247-6887
 Terminal McNamara Gate B7

Twist and Shout — *Snacks* — (734) 857-1300
 Terminal McNamara Central

Vito's Market — *Fast Food*
 Terminal McNamara Gate B18 — (734) 247-6887
 Terminal McNamara Gate C11 — (734) 247-6887

Waterworks Bar and Grill — *American* — (734) 229-0616
 Terminal McNamara Gate A1

West Wings — *Deli* — (734) 955-7055
 Terminal McNamara Gate B5

Wolfgang Puck — *American*
 Terminal Berry Ticketing

EL PASO, TX

Burger King — *Fast Food*
 Lobby FC

Cantina Del Rio — *Mexican*
 Terminal B Gate 2

Carlos and Mickeys Mexican Restaurant — *Mexican*
 Lobby Gate FC

El Paso Vineyards — *Bar*
 Lobby Gate FC

Franklin Express Snackbar and Lounge — *Snacks*
 Terminal A Gate 1

Starbucks — *Coffee*
 Lobby Gate FC

Tortilla Flats Bar and Grill — *Mexican*
 Terminal B Gate 5

FAIRBANKS, AK

The Bush Pilot Lounge — *Bar*

15 Best Airport Restaurants

Upper Level

The Bush Pilot Restaurant   *American*
Upper Level

FLINT, MI

Sullivan's   *Snacks*
Terminal Lobby

Sullivan's Bar   *Bar*
Terminal Gate 6

Sullivan's Restaurant   *American*
Terminal Lobby

FORT LAUDERDALE, FL

Americo's Pizza and Pasta   *Italian*
Terminal 3 Concourse E

Boathouse Bar   *Bar*
Terminal 4 Pre-Security

Boathouse II Bar   *Bar*
Terminal 4 Concourse H

Cheeburger Cheeburger   *Fast Food*
Terminal 1 Concourse B

Chili's Too   *American*
Terminal 3 Pre-Security
Terminal 1 Concourse C

Corky's BBQ and Ribs   *American*
Terminal 3 Concourse F

Cruzan Isle Bar   *Bar*
Terminal 1 Concourse B

Cruzan Rum Bar   *Bar*
Terminal 2 Concourse D

Dunkin Donuts   *Desserts*
Terminal 2 Pre-Security
Terminal 3 Pre-Security

15 Best Airport Restaurants

       Terminal 4 Pre-Security
       Terminal 1 Concourse B
       Terminal 1 Concourse C

Edy's *Desserts*
       Terminal 2 Pre-Security
       Terminal 3 Pre-Security
       Terminal 4 Pre-Security

Grand Forno Bakery *Deli*
       Terminal 2 Concourse D

Kenny Roger's Roasters *American*
       Terminal 2 Concourse D

Keywest Bar and Deli *Bar*
       Terminal 3 Concourse E

La Cucina *Italian*
       Terminal 2 Concourse D

Miami Subs *Deli*
       Terminal 2 Concourse D

Nathan's *Fast Food*
       Terminal 2 Concourse D
       Terminal 4 Concourse H

Pizzeria Uno *Italian*
       Terminal 1 Concourse

Sbarro's *Italian*
       Terminal 4 Pre-Security

Spinaci's Italian *Italian*
       Terminal 1 Concourse C

Tropical Treats *Snacks*
       Terminal 2 Pre-Security
       Terminal 3 Pre-Security

Vito's Deli *Deli*
       Terminal 3 Concourse F

Vito's Market Kiosk *Deli*
       Terminal 1 Pre Security
       Terminal 1 Concourse B
       Terminal 1 Concourse C

15 Best Airport Restaurants

Terminal 3 Concourse E
Terminal 3 Concourse F
Terminal 4 Concourse H

FORT MYERS, FL

Beaches Boardwalk Cafe *American*
Terminal B Gate 2

Books and Sanibel Bean *Coffee*
Terminal B Gate 1
Terminal D Gate 2

Burger King *Fast Food*
Terminal B Gate 5

Casa Bacardi *Bar*
Terminal D Gate 6

Chili's *American*
Terminal Main

Chili's to Go *American*
Terminal Main Gate

Cinnabon *Bakery*
Terminal C Gate 2

Dewar's Club House *Bar*
Terminal C Gate 7

Great American Bagel *Bakery*
Terminal D Gate 2

Maggie's Moo *Desserts*
Terminal B Gate 1

Nathan's *Fast Food*
Terminal Main

Palm City Market *Deli*
Terminal D Gate 6

Quizno's *Deli*
Terminal Main

Sbarro *Fast Food*

15 Best Airport Restaurants

    Terminal C Gate 2

Starbucks   *Coffee*
    Terminal Main
    Terminal B Gate 2
    Terminal D Gate 2

FRESNO, CA

J Muir Tavern   *American*
Terminal Lobby Gate

Starbucks   *Coffee*
    Gate 6
    Lobby

Valley Grill and Sports Bar   *American*
    Gate 14

GRAND RAPIDS, MI

Cinnabon   *Bakery*
    Terminal A
    Terminal B

Fresh Attractions   *Fast Food*
    Terminal A
    Terminal B

Home Turf Sports Grill   *American*
    Grand Hall Gate FC

Pizza Hut Express   *Italian*
    Grand Hall Gate FC

PS AirPub   *Bar*
    Terminal A

Quizno's   *Deli*
    Terminal A

Starbucks   *Coffee*
    Grand Hall Gate FC

HARRISBURG, PA

15 Best Airport Restaurants

Hershey's Ice Cream *Desserts*
    FC

Hudson News and Euro Cafe *Snacks*
    FC

LaVazza Coffee *Coffee*
    FC

McDonald's *Fast Food*
    FC

Starbucks *Coffee*
    Terminal B

The Capital Cafe *American*
    Terminal B

Varsity Grill and Sports Bar *American*
    Lobby 2nd Floor

HONOLULU, HI

Burger King *Fast Food*
    Terminal Gate 12
    Central Terminal
    Interisland Terminal

Chow Mein Express *Oriental*
    Central Terminal Gate
    Interisland Gate

City Deli *Deli*
    Terminal Gate 14

Cocktails *Bar*
    Terminal Gate 6
    Terminal Gate 14
    Terminal Gate 28

Coffee Cart *Coffee*
    Terminal Gate 24

Hot Dog Cart *Fast Food*
    Terminal Gate 29

Ice Cream *Desserts*

15 Best Airport Restaurants

    Terminal Gate 12
    Terminal Gate 14
    Terminal Gate 24
    Terminal Central
    Terminal Interisland

Island Brews — *Bar*
    Terminal Gate 12

Lahaina Chicken — *Regional*
    Terminal Interisland Gate

Noodle Shop — *Oriental*
    Terminal Gate 12

Pizza Hut — *Italian*
    Terminal Gate 6
    Terminal Gate 28
    Central Terminal

Pizza Hut Cart — *Italian*
    Terminal Gate 29

Snack Bar — *Snacks*
    Terminal Gate 6

Starbucks — *Coffee*
    Terminal Gate 12
    Terminal Gate 14
    Central Terminal
    Interisland Terminal Gate

Stinger Rays Bar and Grill — *American*
    Central Terminal

Stinger Rays Bar and Grill — *American*
    Interisland Terminal

HOUSTON (Bush), TX

Auntie Anne's Pretzels — *Snacks*
    Terminal E Gate 12

Bubba's — *American*
    Terminal C North
    Terminal C South

15 Best Airport Restaurants

Bunk House Cafe   *Fast Food*
     Terminal B Gate 84

Burrito Del Sol   *Mexican*
     Terminal C North

Cafe Famiglia   *Coffee*
     Terminal E Gate 18

CC Express   *Coffee*
     Terminal C North
     Terminal C South

Charley's Grilled Subs   *Deli*
     Terminal E Gate 14

Coco Moka   *Desserts*
     Terminal E Gate 2

Coffee Beanery   *Coffee*
     Terminal A North
     Terminal A South

Famous Famiglia   *Italian*
     Terminal E Gate 1

Fit and Fun Yogurt   *Desserts*
     Terminal C North
     Terminal C South

Fox Sports Sky Box   *Bar*
     Terminal E Gate 16

Freshen's   *Desserts*
     Terminal E Gate 3

Harlon's BBQ   *American*
     Terminal B Food Court
     Terminal C North
     Terminal C South

Journey's Lounge   *Bar*
     Terminal A Ticketing Lobby

Le Petit Bistro   *Deli*
     Terminal E Gate 1

Lefty's Passport Grill   *American*

15 Best Airport Restaurants

Terminal D Concourse

Lotus Express *Oriental*
Terminal A Gate South

McDonald's *Fast Food*
Terminal A Gate North
Terminal A Gate South
Terminal B Gate Food Court

Nestle Toll House Cafe *Desserts*
Terminal E Gate 12

Panchito's *Mexican*
Terminal A North
Terminal A South
Terminal B Food Court

Panda Express *Oriental*
Terminal E Gate 1

Papa John's *Italian*
Terminal C North
Terminal C South

Pappadeaux Seafood Kitchen *Seafood*
Terminal E Gate 3

Pappas BBQ *American*
Terminal E Gate 14

Pappasitos Cantina *Mexican*
Terminal E Gate 1

Pizzeria Uno *Italian*
Terminal A South
Terminal B Food Court
Terminal A North

Popcorn Express *Snacks*
Terminal C North
Terminal C South
Terminal D Concourse

Popeye's Chicken *Fast Food*
Terminal C North
Terminal C South

15 Best Airport Restaurants

Primo's
Terminal C South
    Coffee

Riggers
Terminal A South
    Bar

Ruby's Diner
Terminal E Arrivals - Bldg
    American

Schlotzky's
Terminal B Food Court
    Deli

Shipley's Donuts
Terminal B Food Court
    American

Smoothie Factory
Terminal A North
Terminal A South
    Snacks

Smoothie King
Terminal C North
    Snacks

Stadium City Bar and Grill
Terminal A North
    Bar

Starbucks
Terminal C North
Terminal C South
Terminal E Pre-Security
Terminal E Gate 2
Terminal E Gate 14
    Coffee

Subway
Terminal C North
    Deli

Taco Bell
Terminal C South
    Fast Food

Tailwinds
Terminal D Concourse
    Snacks

The Grove
Terminal C North
Terminal A North
Terminal A South
Terminal C South
    Snacks

The Little Creamery
    Desserts

15 Best Airport Restaurants

Terminal E Gate 1

Timeout Concessions *Snacks*
Terminal C North

Wendy's *Fast Food*
Terminal C Gate South
Terminal E Gate 14
Terminal C Gate North

White Magnolia *Fast Food*
Terminal B Gate 68

HOUSTON (Hobby), TX

Barry's Pizza *Italian*
Terminal Central Lobby

Euro Cafe East *Coffee*
Terminal Central Concourse

Euro Cafe West *Coffee*
Terminal Central Concourse

Grab and Go Cafe and Bar *Fast Food*
Terminal Central Concourse
Terminal Central Lobby

Hunans Asian *Oriental*
Terminal Central Lobby

Pappas Burgers *Fast Food*
Terminal Central Concourse

Pappasito's *Mexican*
Terminal Central Concourse

Subway *Deli*
Terminal Central Concourse

Wendy's *Fast Food*
Terminal Central Concourse

INDIANAPOLIS, IN

Asian Chao *Oriental*
Food Court

15 Best Airport Restaurants

Au Bon Pain   *Bakery*
    Food Court

Auntie Anne's   *Snacks*
    Food Court

Budweiser Brewhouse   *Bar*
    Terminal A Gate 84

Caffe Connection   *Coffee*
    Food Court
    Terminal C Gate 33

Caffe Connection   *Coffee*
    Terminal D Gate 5

Charley's Steakery   *Fast Food*
    Food Court

Chick fil A   *Fast Food*
    Food Court

Cinnabon   *Bakery*
    Food Court

Dick Clarks Bandstand   *American*
    Terminal D Gate 3

Fox Sky Box   *American*
    Terminal C Gate 35

Indy Sports Page Pub   *Bar*
    Food Court

Kolache Factory   *Bakery*
    Food Court

La Salsa   *Mexican*
    Food Court

McDonald's   *Fast Food*
    Food Court

Noble Romans   *Italian*
    Food Court

Samuel Adams   *Bar*

Terminal B Gate 42

Smoothie King   *Healthy*
    Terminal B Gate 5
    Terminal A Gate 85
    Terminal A Gate 44

Starbucks   *Coffee*
    Terminal A Gate 81
    Food Court

Subway   *Fast Food*
    Terminal A Gate 78
    Food Court

TGI Fridays   *American*
    Food Court

The Salsalito Bar   *Bar*
    Food Court

JACKSON, MS

On-Stage   *American*

Sports Hall Cafe   *Deli*

Starbucks   *Coffee*

JACKSONVILLE, FL

Big Apple Bagel Deli   *Deli*
    Terminal A

Budweiser Tap Room   *Bar*
    Terminal

Burger King   *Fast Food*
    Food Court

Chilli's Too   *American*
    Food Court

Cinnabon   *Desserts*
    Food Court

15 Best Airport Restaurants

Frankly Gourmet — *Fast Food*
Terminal C

Miller Lite Cafe — *Bar*
Terminal C

Nathans Famous Hot Dogs — *Fast Food*
Food Court

PGA Cafe — *Deli*
Terminal B

Sam Adams — *Bar*
Terminal B

Sam Snead's — *American*
Terminal C

Sbarro's the Italian Eatery — *Italian*
Food Court

Starbucks — *Coffee*
Food Court

Wolfgang Pucks — *American*
Terminal B

KAHULUI, HI

Stinger Rays Bar and Grill — *Bar*
Gate 23

Starbucks — *Coffee*
Baggage Claim

KANSAS CITY, MO

Boulevard Brewery — *American*
Terminal B Gate 56

Budweiser Stadium Club — *Bar*
Terminal C Gate 77

Burger King — *Fast Food*
Terminal B Gate 36

15 Best Airport Restaurants

Cinnabon *Desserts*
   Terminal A Gate 9

Fountains of Seville *American*
   Terminal A Gate 23

Great American Bagel Bakery *Deli*
   Terminal B Gate 32
   Terminal C Gate 32

Great Steak and Potato Company *American*
   Terminal B Gate 56

Home Turf Sports Bar and Grill *American*
   Terminal A Gate 19

Jose Cuervo Tequileria *Mexican*
   Terminal B Gate 36

Just Off Vine *Deli*
   Terminal C Gate 62

Quizno's *Fast food*
   Terminal A Gate 9

Starbucks *Coffee*
   Terminal A Gate 12
   Terminal B Gate 36
   Terminal C Gate 79

LAS VEGAS, NV

Budweiser Brew House *Bar*
   Terminal A

Burger King *Fast Food*
   Terminal A

Carry Out Carry On *Deli*
   Terminal A

Chili's Too *American*
   Terminal A

Cinnabon *Desserts*
   Terminal A
   Terminal B
   Terminal C

15 Best Airport Restaurants

    Terminal D
    Terminal 2

Flatbreadz   *Italian*
    Terminal A

Hot Dog City   *Fast Food*
    Terminal A

Mrs. Field's Cookies   *Desserts*
    Terminal A

Pretzelmaker   *Snacks*
    Terminal A

Starbucks   *Coffee*
    Terminal A

TCBY   *Desserts*
    Terminal A

Vienna Beef   *Fast Food*
    Terminal A

LEXINGTON, KY

Bourbon Bar   *American*
    2nd Floor

Creative Croissants Cafe and Spirits   *Deli*
    Terminal

LITTLE ROCK, AR

Andina's   *Coffee*
    FC

Burger King   *Fast Food*
    FC

Frankly Gourmet   *Deli*
    Gate 4

Fresh Attractions   *Deli*
    FC

Ouachita Brew House   *Bar*
   FC

Pizza Hut   *Italian*
   FC

RiverBend Bar and Grill   *American*
   Lobby

TCBY   *Desserts*
   FC

LONG BEACH, CA

Daugherty's Cafe   *Deli*
   Terminal

Grab and Go Kiosks   *Deli*
   Terminal

Legends of Aviation Restaurant and Bar   *American*
   Terminal

LOS ANGELES, CA

Arrival Cafe   *American*
   Terminal International   310-215-4215

Backlot Deli   *Deli*
   Terminal 1   (310) 215-5163

Boudin Sourdough Bakery   *Deli*
   Terminal 7   (310) 646-4471
   Terminal 2   (310) 646-4471

Brioche Doree *Deli*
   Terminal 4   (310) 342-0497

Bud Tap Room *Bar*
   Terminal International   (310) 215-4205

Burger King   *Fast Food*
   Terminal 2   (310) 646-4680
   Terminal 8   (310) 646-4471
   Terminal 3   (310) 646-6476
   Terminal 4   (310) 646-3478

15 Best Airport Restaurants

California Pizza Kitchen
    Terminal 8 Departure Level
    Terminal 5 Departure Level

American
(310) 646-6474
(310) 417-1908

Chili's Too
    Terminal 4 Departure Level

American
(310) 646-3478

Cinnabon
    International
    Terminal 6

Desserts
(310) 215-4214
310-215-4215

City Deli
    Terminal 2

Deli
310-646-3475

Creative Croissants
    Terminal 5

Deli
310-216-0989

Daily Grill
    International

American
310-215-5180

Diedrich Coffee
    International

Coffee
(310) 215-4205

Eaturna
    Terminal 1

Deli
(310) 646-0734

El Cholo Cantina
    Terminal 5
    Terminal 1
    International

Mexican
(310) 417-1910
(310) 645-9984
(310) 645-2502

Encounter Restaurant
    Theme Building

American
(310) 215-5151

Jody Maroni's
    Terminal 3
    Terminal 6

Fast Food
(310) 646-8056
(310) 646-4455

Karl Strauss Microbrewery
    Terminal 7

Bar
(310) 646-4471

LA Roadhouse Route 66 *American*
    Terminal 2
    Terminal 8

(310) 646-4680
(310) 641-9235

La Salsa
    Terminal 7

Mexican
310-646-6470

15 Best Airport Restaurants

Malibu Al's   *Fast Food*
    Terminal 5   (310) 417-1912

Manhattan Beach Brewing Company   *Bar*
    Terminal 4   (310) 646-4471

Marina Bar   *Bar*
    International   310-215-4205

McDonald's   *Fast Food*
    Terminal 7   (310) 410-5157
    Terminal 5   (310) 670-9830
    Terminal 1   (310) 410-5161
    International   (310) 670-9364

Monet's a California Deli   *Deli*
    Terminal 6   310-215-4212

Northside Bar   *Bar*
    International Gate 121   (310) 215-4203

Redondo Beach Brewing Co.   *Bar*
    Terminal 6   310-646-4455

Ruby's   *American*
    Terminal 6   310-646-2480

Seattle's Best Coffee   *Coffee*
    Terminal International   (310) 215-4215

Starbucks   *Coffee*
    Terminal 1   (310) 646-4471
    Terminal 2
    Terminal 3
    Terminal 4
    Terminal 6
    Terminal 7
    Terminal 8

Sushi Boy   *Oriental*
    International   310-342-7070

Travel Right Cafe   *American*
    Terminal 4   (310) 665-0208

Wolfgang Puck   *American*
    Terminal 7   (310) 215-5169

15 Best Airport Restaurants

Terminal 2   (310) 215-5166

LOUISVILLE, KY

Burger King *Fast Food*
   Terminal Mall

Home Team Sports Bar *Bar*
   Terminal A Gate 5

Kentucky Fired Chicken *Fast Food*
   Terminal Mall

Pizza Hut *Italian*
   Terminal Mall

Quizno's *Deli*
   Terminal B Gate 9

Starbucks *Coffee*
   Terminal Mall

Waterfront Bar and Grill *American*
   Terminal B Gate 9

Woodford Reserve Grill *American*
   Terminal Mall

LUBBOCK, TX

Burger King *Fast Food*
   Food Court

HMS Deli *Deli*
   Food Court

HMS Lounge *Bar*
   Food Court

Pizza Hut *Italian*
   Food Court

Starbucks *Bar*
   Food Court

TCBY *Desserts*
   Food Court

15 Best Airport Restaurants

MADISON, WI

Ancora Coffee Roasters — *Coffee*
Gate 7

Ben and Jerry's Ice Cream — *Desserts*
Gate 7

Caffe Ritazza — *Coffee*
Lobby

Great Dane Brew Pub — *American*
Gate 7

Quizno's — *Deli*
Gate 7

UNO Chicago Pizza — *Italian*
Gate 7

Usingers Wurst German Bar — *Deli*
Gate 5

MEMPHIS, TN

Arby's — *Fast Food*
Ticketing

Back Yard Burgers — *Regional*
Ticketing

Blue Note Cafe — *Bar*
Ticketing

Coffee Beanery — *Coffee*
Terminal A Gate 21
Ticketing

Corky's BBQ — *Regional*
Terminal A Gate 25
Terminal C Gate 3

Edy's — *Desserts*
Terminal B Gate 40
Terminal B Gate 4

15 Best Airport Restaurants

Einstein Bros Bagels — *Deli*
Terminal C Gate 14

Grisanti's Bol a Pasta — *Italian*
Terminal A Gate 11

Jim Neely's Interstate BarBQue — *Regional*
Terminal B Gate 16

Juice It Up — *Healthy*
Ticketing

Lenny's — *Deli*
Terminal B Gate 3

Maggie O'Shea's — *Bar*
Ticketing

Rhythm's Cafe and Bar — *Regional*
Terminal B Gate 35

Starbucks — *Coffee*
Terminal A Gate 20
Terminal C Gate 16

Varsity Grill — *American*
Terminal C Gate 11

Vito's Market — *Deli*
Terminal A Gate 5

MIAMI, FL

Americas Favorite Ice Cream — *Desserts*
Terminal E Pre Security

Au Bon Pain — *Deli*
Terminal A Pre Security
Terminal G Pre Security

Budweiser Brew House — *Bar*
Terminal G Post Security
Terminal H Post Security
Terminal F Food Court

Burger King — *Fast Food*

15 Best Airport Restaurants

    Terminal D Post Security
    Terminal E Pre Security
    Terminal F Food Court
    Terminal G Post Security

Cafe Versailles *Deli*
    Terminal A Post Security
    Terminal D Food Court
    Terminal D Pre Security
    Terminal E Post Security
    Terminal F Pre Security
    Terminal H Pre Security

California Pizza Kitchen *American*
    Terminal E Pre Security

Casa Bacardi *Mexican*
    Terminal E Pre Security

Chicago Pizza *Italian*
    Terminal D Post Security

Chili's *American*
    Terminal G Pre Security

Chili's To Go *American*
    Terminal E Post Security
    Terminal F Pre Security
    Terminal G Post Security

Cinnabon *Desserts*
    Terminal H Post Security

Cozzoli's Pizzeria *Italian*
    Terminal G Pre Security

Dunkin Donuts *Desserts*
    Terminal F Pre Security

Fresh Attractions To Go *Fast Food*
    Terminal D Security

Guava and Java *Coffee*
    Terminal F Security
    Terminal G Security

Home Turf Sports Bar *Bar*
    Terminal E Post Security

15 Best Airport Restaurants

Islander Bar and Grill   *Bar*
    Terminal D Post Security

Jet Bar Havana   *Bar*
    Terminal D Pre Security

Jose Cuervo   *Bar*
    Terminal A Post Security

La Carreta   *Mexican*
    Terminal D Post Security
    Terminal E Pre Security

Manchu Wok   *Oriental*
    Terminal D Food Court

Nathans   *Fast Food*
    Terminal E Post Security

Pizza Hut   *Italian*
    Terminal E Post Security

Pizza Hut Express   *Italian*
    Terminal A Pre Security
    Terminal F Food Court
    Terminal G Post Security

Quizno's   *Italian*
    Terminal H Gate Post Security

Sam Adams Bar   *Bar*
    Terminal D Post Security

Sam Adams Brewhouse   *Bar*
    Terminal E Post Security

Sbarro   *Italian*
    Terminal F Gate Pre Security

Smoothie Company   *Deli*
    Terminal D Post Security

Starbucks   *Coffee*
    Terminal A Pre Security
    Terminal A Post Security
    Terminal C Pre Security
    Terminal D Post Security

15 Best Airport Restaurants

Terminal E Post Security
Terminal E Pre Security
Terminal H Post Security

Sushi Bar *Oriental*
Terminal E Pre Security

The Great American Bagel Bakery *Deli*
Terminal E Pre Security

Top of the Port Restaurant *American*
Terminal E Hotel

Villa Pizza *Italian*
Terminal D Food Court

MILWAUKEE, WI

Big Apple Bagels *Bakery*
Terminal D

Brats *Regional*
Terminal E
Terminal C

Burger King *Fast Food*
Terminal Food Court

Cinnabon *Bakery*
Terminal Food Court

Fruit Smoothies *Healthy*
Terminal D

Miller Brewhouse *Bar*
Terminal Food Court

Mitchell's Cafe *American*
Terminal Food Court

Pizza Hut *Italian*
Terminal Food Court
Terminal E
Terminal C

Pizzaria Uno *Italian*
Terminal D

15 Best Airport Restaurants

Quizno's　　　　　　　　　　　　　　　　*Deli*
　　Terminal C

Starbucks　　　　　　　　　　　　　　　*Coffee*
　　Terminal Food Court
　　Terminal D

TCBY *Desserts*
　　Terminal D

Usinger's Deli　　　　　　　　　　　　　*Deli*
　　Terminal Food Court

Wolfgang Puck　　　　　　　　　　　　*American*
　　Terminal D

MINNEAPOLIS, MN

360 Gourmet Burrito　　　　　　　　　　*Mexican*
　　Terminal Lindbergh Checkpoint 3　　　612-726-9360

A&W　　　　　　　　　　　　　　　　　*Fast Food*
　　Terminal Lindbergh C-12　　　　　　　612-727-3388
　　Terminal Lindbergh Gate 1　　　　　　612-727-1498

Axel's Bonfire　　　　　　　　　　　　　*American*
　　Terminal Lindbergh Checkpoint 3　　　612-726-5360

Ben and Jerry's　　　　　　　　　　　　*Desserts*
　　Terminal Lindbergh Gate Checkpoint 4　612-970-2933

Burger King　　　　　　　　　　　　　　*Fast Food*
　　Terminal Lindbergh Gate E-3　　　　　612-726-5360
　　Terminal Lindbergh Gate F-6　　　　　612-726-5360
　　Terminal Lindbergh Gate Checkpoint 4　612-726-5360

California Pizza Kitchen　　　　　　　　*American*
　　Terminal Lindbergh Gate F-6　　　　　612-726-5360

Caribou Coffee　　　　　　　　　　　　*Coffee*
　　Terminal Humphrey Baggage Claim　　612-726-6289
　　Terminal Lindbergh Gate E-5　　　　　612-726-1165
　　Terminal Lindbergh Gate F-1　　　　　612-727-1750
　　Terminal Lindbergh Gate G-1　　　　　612-727-1653
　　Terminal Lindbergh Checkpoint 4　　　612-726-9305

15 Best Airport Restaurants

Charley's Philly Grill — *Fast Food*
    Terminal Lindbergh Checkpoint — 612-727-1849

Chili's Too — *American*
    Terminal Lindbergh G-17 — 612-726-5360
    Terminal Lindbergh Checkpoint 5 — 612-726-5360

D'Amico and Sons Cafe — *Deli*
    Terminal Lindbergh Gate E-15 — 612-726-5378

DQ Grill and Chill — *American*
    Terminal Lindbergh Gate 6 — 612-726-6271

Dunn Bros Coffee — *Coffee*
    Terminal Lindbergh Gate C-12 — 612-727-3388
    Terminal Humphrey Near Security — 612-727-1213

Einstein Bros Bagels — *Deli*
    Terminal Lindbergh Gate C-12 — 612-727-3388

Famous Famiglia — *American*
    Terminal Lindbergh Checkpoint 4 — 612-727-1849

Fletcher's Wharf — *American*
    Terminal Humphrey Gate Near Security — 612-727-1213

French Meadow Bakery — *Deli*
    Terminal Lindbergh Gate F-3 — 612-726-5360
    Terminal Lindbergh Checkpoint 1 — 612-726-5360

Godfather's Pizza — *Italian*
    Terminal Lindbergh Gate C-12 — 612-727-3388
    Terminal Lindbergh Gate A-1 — 612-727-1498

Grandaddy's Bar — *Bar*
    Terminal Humphrey Gate Near Security — 612-727-1213

Great River Market and Deli — *American*
    Terminal Lindbergh Gate G-13 — 612-726-5360

Harvest Market — *Deli*
    Terminal Humphrey Gate Near Security — 612-727-1213

Icescape — *American*
    Terminal Lindbergh Gate E-9 — 612-726-5362

Ike's Food and Cocktails — *American*
    Terminal Lindbergh Checkpoint 1 — 612-726-5360

15 Best Airport Restaurants

Itasca Grille
　　Terminal Lindbergh Gate A-1
American
612-727-1007

Locanda D Amico
　　Terminal Lindbergh Gate F-1
Italian
612-726-5360

Market to Go
　　Terminal Lindbergh Gate G-16
Snacks
612-726-5360

Maui Taco
　　Terminal Lindbergh Gate C-6
Mexican
612-727-3388

McDonald's
　　Terminal Lindbergh Gate G-1
　　Terminal Lindbergh Gate G-18
　　Terminal Lindbergh Gate G-18
Fast Food
612-726-6480
612-726-6480
612-726-6480

Northern Lights Grill
　　Terminal Lindbergh Gate Entrance
American
612-726-5360

O Gara's Restaurant
　　Terminal Lindbergh Gate F-12
Regional

Quizno's
　　Terminal Lindbergh Gate D-1
　　Terminal Lindbergh Gate G-18
　　Terminal Lindbergh Gate A-1
Fast Food
612-726-5360
612-726-5360
612-727-1498

Rock Bottom Restaurant
　　Terminal Lindbergh Gate C-D Intersect
Bar
612-726-5360

Rocky Mountain Chocolate Factory
　　Terminal Lindbergh Checkpoint 1
Desserts
612-726-9133

Sbarro
　　Terminal Lindbergh Gate E-9
　　Terminal Lindbergh Gate C-2
Fast Food
612-726-5360
612-726-5360

Skål Cafe and Bar
　　Terminal Lindbergh Gate A-10
Bar
612-726-6354

Stage Deli
　　Terminal Lindbergh Checkpoint 1
Deli
612-970-2933

Starbucks
　　Terminal Lindbergh Gate C-1
　　Terminal Lindbergh Baggage Claim
Coffee
612-726-5360
612-726-5360

15 Best Airport Restaurants

    Terminal Lindbergh Gate G-16   612-726-5360
    Terminal Lindbergh Checkpoint 1   612-726-5360

Subway   *Fast Food*
    Terminal Lindbergh Gate G-1   612-727-1774

Surf Bar   *Bar*
    Terminal Lindbergh Gate C-6   612-727-3388

Tequileria   *Mexican*
    Terminal Lindbergh Gate G-9   612-726-5630

TGI Fridays   *American*
    Terminal Lindbergh Gate C-12   612-970-7800

The Lodge   *Bar*
    Terminal Lindbergh Gate G-3   612-726-5360

Varsity Sports Bar and Deli   *American*
    Terminal Lindbergh Gate B-Tunnel   612-726-6390

Wok and Roll *Oriental*
    Terminal Lindbergh Gate C-12   612-726-1999
    Terminal Lindbergh Gate E-5   612-727-2579
    Terminal Lindbergh Gate Checkpoint 4   612-726-1999

Wolfgang Puck   *American*
    Terminal Lindbergh Gate G-7   612-726-5360

ZYNG Noodlery   *Oriental*
    Terminal Lindbergh Gate G-4   612-726-5360

NASHVILLE, TN

AirMeals   *Fast Food*
    Terminal B Gate 5

Andrew Jacksons Tavern   *Bar*
    North Terminal Lounge

Cantina Tio Luis   *Mexican*
    Terminal B Gate 4

Capitol Hill Grille   *American*
    Terminal Connector

Chicago Pizzeria Uno   *Italian*

15 Best Airport Restaurants

Lobby Post Security

Coffee Beanery — *Coffee*
Terminal C Gate 10

Market Deli — *Deli*
Terminal B Gate 3

Market Street Pub — *Bar*
Terminal C Food Court

Miami Express — *Deli*
Terminal C Food Court

Pasta with Pizzazz — *Italian*
Terminal C Gate 14

The Bull Pen and Stadium Club — *American*
Terminal C Gate 20

The Landing — *American*
Terminal Lobby Post Security

Whitt's Barbecue — *Regional*
Terminal A
Terminal B
Terminal C

NEW ORLEANS, LA

Acme Oyster House — *Regional*
Ticket Lobby

Airdogs — *Fast Food*
Terminal C Gate 36
Terminal D Gate 42

Atrium Lounge — *Bar*
Terminal C Gate 34

Austin Blues — *Regional*
Terminal A Gate 3

Big Easy Lounge — *Bar*
Ticket Lobby

Blue Bell — *Desserts*

15 Best Airport Restaurants

    Terminal B Gate 15
    Terminal C Gate 37
    Ticket Lobby

Creole Carvery   *Regional*
    Terminal C Gate 30

Creole Kitchen   *Regional*
    Ticket Lobby

Crescent City Snacks   *Snacks*
    Terminal D Gate 43

Cruzan's Rum Bar   *Bar*
    Terminal B Gate 20

Garden District Bistro   *Bar*
    Terminal A Gate 4

Grove   *Snacks*
    Terminal A Gate 6
    Terminal B Gate 13
    Terminal C Gate 28
    Terminal D Gate 40

Hot Pops   *Fast Food*
    Terminal A Gate 5
    Terminal C Gate 27

Jester's Bar and Grill   *Bar*
    Terminal D Gate 38

Jester's Express   *Fast Food*
    Terminal B Gate 21

Live Oaks Bar   *Bar*
    Terminal B Gate 19

Lucky Dog   *Fast Food*
    Terminal B Gate 17
    Terminal A Gate 7

Pizza to Go   *Italian*
    Terminal C Gate 34

PJ's Coffee   *Coffee*
    Ticket Lobby

15 Best Airport Restaurants

Popeye's — *Regional*
  Ticket Lobby

Praline Connection — *Desserts*
  Terminal B Gate 12
  Terminal B Gate 16

Subway — *Fast Food*
  Terminal B Gate 14

Yogurt — *Healthy*
  Terminal C Gate 31

NEWPORT NEWS, VA

Blue Sky Cafe — *Deli*
  Gate 2

TK's Pub — *Bar*
  Gate 2

NEW YORK (Kennedy), NY

7th Avenue Deli — *Deli*
  Terminal 7 Food Court

Antonio's — *Italian*
  Terminal 7 Food Court

Atlantic Bar and Grille — *American*
  Terminal 7 Gate 2

Au Bon Pain — *Deli*
  Terminal 4 Arrivals
  Terminal 4 Mezzanine - East
  Terminal 4 Gate B23
  Terminal 8 Pre-Security
  Terminal 8 Gate 23
  Terminal 9 Gate 35

Aunt Butchies — *Desserts*
  Terminal 6 Gate 7

Away Cafe *American*
  Terminal 6 Pre-Security

15 Best Airport Restaurants

Bananas Ultimate Juice Bar *Deli*
    Terminal 8 Pre-Security

Boars Head Deli *Deli*
    Terminal 6 Food Court
    Terminal 8 Gate Pre-Security

Broadway Brewing *Bar*
    Terminal 8 Gate 8
    Terminal 8 Pre-Security
    Terminal 8 Gate 23

Brooklyn Ale House *Bar*
    Terminal 4 Gate B26

Brooklyn Beer Garden *Bar*
    Terminal 1 Gate 5

Brooklyn National Deli *Deli*
    Terminal 9 Gate 40

Burger King *Fast Food*
    Terminal 2 Food Court
    Terminal 3 Gate 18

CafÃ© Ritazza *Italian*
    Terminal 4 Mezzanine – West

Chee Burger Chee Burger *Fast Food*
    Terminal 6 Food Court

Chili's To Go Kiosk *American*
    Terminal 3 Gate 18

Chili's Too *American*
    Terminal 3 Food Court

Cibo Express *Deli*
    Terminal 5 Gate 18
    Terminal 5 Gate 23
    Terminal 6 Gate 1
    Terminal 6 Gate 7

Cibo Express Kiosk *Deli*
    Terminal 6 Baggage Claim
    Terminal 6 Gate 12
    Terminal 6 Gate 9

Create Your Own Salad *Fast Food*

15 Best Airport Restaurants

Terminal 6 Food Court

Creative Croissants   *Fast Food*
    Terminal 2 Gate 21
    Terminal 2 Food Court

Cucina Sandwiches and Salads   *Deli*
    Terminal 4 Gate Mezzanine – West

Deep Blue Sushi   *Oriental*
    Terminal 6 Gate 9

Dunkin Donuts   *Desserts*
    Terminal 3 Food Court
    Terminal 6 Gate 10
    Terminal 8 Pre-Security

Dunkin Donuts Kiosk   *Desserts*
    Terminal 6 Pre-Security
    Terminal 9 Pre-Security

Edy's Kiosk   *Desserts*
    Terminal 2 Gate 21

Euro CafZ   *Deli*
    Terminal 1 Food Court
    Terminal 9 Gate 42

Everything Yogurt   *Desserts*
    Terminal 8 Gate Pre-Security

Famous Famiglia Pizzeria   *Italian*
    Terminal 6 Gate 10

Great American Bagel   *Snacks*
    Terminal 3 Food Court

Greenwich Village Bistro   *Deli*
    Terminal 1 Food Court

Gretels and Pretzels   *Snacks*
    Terminal 8 Pre-Security

I Can't Believe Its Yogurt   *Desserts*
    Terminal 6 Pre-Security

KFC Express   *Fast Food*
    Terminal 4 Mezzanine - West

15 Best Airport Restaurants

Krispy Kreme Kiosk *Desserts*
    Terminal 1 Food Court

Latitudes *Deli*
    Terminal 7 Food Court

Links on Tap *Bar*
    Terminal 2 Food Court
    Terminal 2 Gate 21

Manchu Wok *Oriental*
    Terminal 3 Food Court

Maui Wowi *Coffee*
    Terminal 6 Food Court

McDonald's *Fast Food*
    Terminal 1 Food Court
    Terminal 4 Mezzanine - East
    Terminal 7 Food Court
    Terminal 8 Pre-Security

Mex and the City *Mexican*
    Terminal 6 Food Court

More Than Sweets *Snacks*
    Terminal 3 Gate 11

Napa Valley Wine Bar *Bar*
    Terminal 1 Gate 3

Nathan's Hot Dogs *Fast Food*
    Terminal 8 Pre-Security

NY Sports Bar and Grill *Bar*
    Terminal 6 Gate 9

Panini Express *Italian*
    Terminal 1 Gate 2
    Terminal 1 Food Court

Panini Express Kiosk *Italian*
    Terminal 1 Gate 8

Papaya King *Fast Food*
    Terminal 6 Gate 7

15 Best Airport Restaurants

Peet's Coffee   *Coffee*
    Terminal 7 Pre-Security
    Terminal 7 Gate 6

Salad CafZ   *Deli*
    Terminal 8 Gate Pre-Security

Sam Adams Brewhouse   *Bar*
    Terminal 3 Food Court
    Terminal 3 Gate 18

Sam Adams Brewhouse Kiosk   *Bar*
    Terminal 3 Gate 18

Sam Adams Celebrates NY   *Bar*
    Terminal 4 Mezzanine – West

Sbarro   *Italian*
    Terminal 8 Pre-Security
    Terminal 3 Food Court
    Terminal 4 Mezzanine – East

Seattle's Best   *Coffee*
    Terminal 7 Pre-Security
    Terminal 7 Gate 6

Shannon's Bar   *Bar*
    Terminal 4 Gate A3

Sky Asian Bistro   *Deli*
    Terminal 6 Gate Food Court

SoHo Bistro   *Deli*
    Terminal 9 Gate 44

Soup & Kimbob   *Oriental*
    Terminal 1 Food Court

Starbucks   *Coffee*
    Terminal 2 Gate 24
    Terminal 3 Food Court
    Terminal 3 Gate 18
    Terminal 9 Gate 45

Starbucks Kiosk   *Coffee*
    Terminal 2 Food Court

Subway *Deli*

15 Best Airport Restaurants

    Terminal 7 Pre-Security

TCBY   *Desserts*
    Terminal 3 Gate Food Court

The Grove *Snacks*
    Terminal 6 Pre-Security
    Terminal 7 Food Court
    Terminal 8 Gate 6
    Terminal 8 Gate 23

Treat Street Kiosk   *Snacks*
    Terminal 8 Gate 3

Tuscany Cafe   *Italian*
    Terminal 1 Lufthansa

Wok and Roll   *Oriental*
    Terminal 2 Food Court
    Terminal 1 Food Court
    Terminal 2 Gate 21
    Terminal 4 Mezzanine - West
    Terminal 8 Pre-Security

NEW YORK (La Guardia), NY

Asian Chao *Oriental*
    Terminal Central Pre-Security

Au Bon Pain   *Deli*
    Terminal Central Gate Pre-Security
    Terminal Central Gate C3
    Terminal Central Gate A3
    Terminal Central Gate B3

Auntie Anne's   *Snacks*
    Terminal Central Gate C3
    Terminal Central Gate A3
    Terminal Central Gate B5
    Terminal Central Gate D2

Baskin Robbins   *Desserts*
    Terminal Central Pre-Security

Big Apple Bar   *Bar*
    Terminal US Air Shuttle Food Court

15 Best Airport Restaurants

Brooklyn National Deli   *Deli*
    Terminal Central Pre-Security

Burger King   *Fast Food*
    Terminal Delta Food Court

Chili's Too   *American*
    Terminal Delta Fast Food

Cibo Bar   *Bar*
    Terminal US Airways Food Court

Cibo Express   *Deli*
    Terminal US Airways Food Court
    Terminal Central Gate C5
    Terminal Central Gate B5
    Terminal US Air Shuttle Pre-Security
    Terminal US Air Shuttle Food Court

Coffee Beanery   *Coffee*
    Terminal Central Pre-Security

Dunkin Donuts   *Desserts*
    Terminal Central Pre-Security
    Terminal Central Gate B6
    Terminal US Air Shuttle Pre-Security

Dunkin Donuts Express   *Desserts*
    Terminal US Airways Food Court

Euro Cafe   *Deli*
    Terminal US Air Shuttle Food Court

Famous Famiglia   *Italian*
    Terminal Central Pre-Security

Figs CafZ   *American*
    Terminal Central Gate D4

Figs Restaurant   *American*
    Terminal Central Gate Pre-Security

Fox Sports Bar and Restaurant   *Bar*
    Terminal Delta Gate 2

ICBIY   *Desserts*
    Terminal Delta Gate Pre-Security
    Terminal Delta

15 Best Airport Restaurants

Jet Rock Bar and Grill — *Bar*
    Terminal Central Pre-Security

Joeys Pizza — *Italian*
    Terminal US Airways Food Court

McDonald's — *Fast Food*
    Terminal US Airways Food Court

Nathan's — *Fast Food*
    Terminal Delta Gate 2

New York Sports Bar — *Bar*
    Terminal Central Pre-Security
    Terminal Central Gate B1

Papaya King — *Fast Food*
    Terminal US Airways Food Court

Sam Adams — *Bar*
    Terminal Central Gate D10

Sbarro Express — *Italian*
    Terminal Delta Food Court

Sky Asian Bistro — *Oriental*
    Terminal US Airways Food Court

Slip Mahoney's — *American*
    Terminal US Airways Food Court

Starbucks — *Coffee*
    Terminal Delta

The Grove — *Snacks*
    Terminal Delta Pre-Security
    Terminal Delta Gate Area

Wendy's — *Fast Food*
    Terminal Central Pre-Security

NEW YORK (NEWARK), NY

Americo's — *American*
    Terminal C Gate 109

15 Best Airport Restaurants

Asian Chao *American*
Terminal B Gate Pre Security

Au Bon Pain *Deli*
Terminal C Gate 70

A&W All American Food *Fast Food*
Terminal C Food Court

Ben and Jerry's *Desserts*
Terminal C Food Court

Borders CafZ *Mexican*
Terminal C Gate 3

Brooklyn Brewery Jazz Bar *Bar*
Terminal C Food Court

Budweiser Brew House *Bar*
Terminal A Gate 2
Terminal C Gate 73

Burger King *Fast Food*
Terminal A Pre Security

CafZ Ritazza *Italian*
Terminal C Bag Claim 2

Carvel Ice Cream *Desserts*
Terminal B Gate 1

Central Market Grill *American*
Terminal A Pre Security

Cereality Cereal Bar *Snacks*
Terminal A Gate 1
Terminal A Gate 2
Terminal B Gate 1

Charley's Steakery *American*
Terminal B Pre Security

Chili's To Go *American*
Terminal B Pre Security

Dick Clark's American Bandstand *American*
Terminal A Gate 39

15 Best Airport Restaurants

Dunkin Donuts *Desserts*
    Terminal A Pre Security
    Terminal C Food Court

Euro CafZ *Deli*
    Terminal C Bag Claim 9

Famous Famiglia *Italian*
    Terminal A Pre Security
    Terminal C Food Court

Formaggios CafZ *Italian*
    Terminal B Pre Security

Gallagher's Steakhouse *American*
    Terminal C Gate 3

Garden State Deli and Bar *Bar*
    Terminal A Gate 3

Garden State Diner *American*
    Terminal C Gate 81

Great American Bagel Bakery *Deli*
    Terminal A Pre Security

Greenleaf's Grille *American*
    Terminal C Food Court

Host Coffee *Coffee*
    Terminal B Gate 2

I Can't Believe Its Yogurt *Desserts*
    Terminal A Gate 2

Jake's Coffee House *Coffee*
    Terminal C Gate 75
    Terminal C Gate 109

Le Petit Bistro *Deli*
    Terminal C Gate

Maui Taco *Oriental*
    Terminal C Food Court

McDonald's *Fast Food*
    Terminal B Pre Security
    Terminal C Food Court

15 Best Airport Restaurants

Miami Subs Grille — *Deli*
　　Terminal C Gate C2

Miller Brew House — *Bar*
　　Terminal C2 Gate 103

Nathan's — *Fast Food*
　　Terminal C1 Food Court

Natural Island Kiosk — *Snacks*
　　Terminal C1 Gate 71

O'Brien's Grille and Pub — *Bar*
　　Terminal B Gate 1

Out of Bounds Sports Bar — *Bar*
　　Terminal C1 Gate 82

Pizza Uno — *Italian*
　　Terminal A Gate 2

Pizza Uno Express — *Italian*
　　Terminal B Gate 1

Rio Douro Cafe — *Mexican*
　　Terminal C1 Food Court

Sam Adams — *Bar*
　　Terminal B Gate 2
　　Terminal B Gate 3

Sam Adams Brewhouse — *Bar*
　　Terminal C2 Gate112

Sarku — *Oriental*
　　Terminal C3 Food Court

Sbarro — *Italian*
　　Terminal C1 Gate 80
　　Terminal C1 Food Court

Seattle's Best Coffee — *Coffee*
　　Terminal A Gate Pre Security
　　Terminal A Gate 3
　　Terminal B Gate 1

Splendid Treats — *Desserts*

15 Best Airport Restaurants

    Terminal C3 Food Court

Stage Deli   *Deli*
    Terminal B Gate Pre Security

Starbucks   *Coffee*
    Terminal A Pre Security
    Terminal A Gate 2
    Terminal A Gate 1
    Terminal B Pre Security
    Terminal C Pre Security
    Terminal C3 Connector

Steak Escape   *American*
    Terminal C3 Food Court

Subway   *Deli*
    Terminal A Pre Security

Surf City Squeeze   *Snacks*
     Terminal C3 Food Court

TCBY   *Desserts*
    Terminal C3 Food Court

TGI Fridays   *American*
    Terminal A Gate Pre Security
    Terminal A Gate 1

The Grove   *Snacks*
    Terminal A Pre Security
    Terminal A Gate 2
    Terminal C Bag Claim 6
    Terminal C1 Gate 83
    Terminal C1 Gate 95
    Terminal C3 Connector

Treat Street   *Desserts*
    Terminal C1 Food Court
    Terminal C1 Connector

Villa Pizza   *Italian*
    Terminal B Pre Security

Vito's Deli   *Italian*
    Terminal C2 Gate 103

Wetzel's Pretzels   *Snacks*

15 Best Airport Restaurants

Terminal B Gate 1

Wok and Roll *Oriental*
Terminal A Pre Security
Terminal C1 Gate 90
Terminal C1 Food Court

Wolfgang Puck Snacks *Snacks*
Terminal B Gate 3

NORFOLK, VA

A&W *Fast Food*
Terminal Main

American Bagel Bakery *Bakery*
Terminal B

Freshens *Desserts*
Terminal Main

Phillips Seafood Restaurant *American*
Terminal Main

Starbucks *Coffee*
Terminal Main

The Raceway Grill *Fast Food*
Terminal B

The Varsity Grill *Deli*
Terminal Main

The Virginia Nut Company *Snacks*
Terminal Main

UNOS Chicago Grill *Italian*
Terminal Main

UNOS Pizza *Italian*
Terminal A

USS Norfolk *Bar*
Terminal A

Wolfgang Puck To Go *American*
Terminal A

15 Best Airport Restaurants

Terminal B

OAKLAND, CA

360 Degree Gourmet Burritos — *Mexican*
Terminal 1

Andale — *Fast Food*
Terminal 2

Bay Bridge Bar and Deli — *Deli*
Terminal 1

Bay Cafe — *American*
Terminal 2

CPK ASAP — *Deli*
Terminal 2

Destination OAK — *American*
Terminal 2

Fenton's Ice Cream — *Desserts*
Terminal 2

Freshens — *Desserts*
Terminal 1

Gordon Biersch — *Bar*
Terminal 2

Juice It Up — *Snacks*
Terminal 2

Knights Cafe — *American*
Terminal 1

Market Fresh — *Snacks*
Terminal 2

Max's — *Bar*
Terminal 2

Quarter Pound Giant Burger — *Fast Food*
Terminal 1

Round Table Pizza — *Italian*

15 Best Airport Restaurants

Terminal 1

Round Table Pizza — *Italian*
Terminal 2

Starbucks — *Coffee*
Terminal 2

Training Grounds — *American*
Terminal 2

ONTARIO, CA

Applebee's Grill — *American*
Terminal 2

California Speedway Cafe — *American*
Terminal 4

Carl's Jr — *Fast Food*
Terminal 2
Terminal 4

El Paseo — *Mexican*
Terminal 2
Terminal 4

Jake's Bar and Deli — *Bar*
Terminal 2
Terminal 4

Jake's Coffee House — *Coffee*
Terminal 2
Terminal 4

Juice It Up — *Healthy*
Terminal 2
Terminal 4

Round Table Pizza — *Italian*
Terminal 2
Terminal 4

ORLANDO (Int'l), FL

Carvel — *Desserts*

15 Best Airport Restaurants

Food Court (407) 851-1334

Chick fil A *Fast Food*
Food Court (407) 851-1334

Chili's Too *American*
West Hall (407) 851-1334

Fox Sports Sky Box *Bar*
West Hall (407) 851-1334

Fresh Attractions Deli *Deli*
Food Court (407) 851-1334

Hemispheres *American*
East Hall (407) 825-1234

Krispy Kreme *Desserts*
Food Court (407) 851-1334

Macaroni Grill *Italian*
West Hall (407) 851-1334

McCoy's Bar and Grill *American*
Hyatt (407) 825-1234

McDonald's *Fast Food*
Food Court (407) 825-7331

Nathan's *Fast Food*
Food Court (407) 851-1334

Sbarro *Italian*
Food Court (407) 851-1334

Seattle's Best Coffee *Coffee*
West Hall (407) 825-6683

Zyng's Asian Grill *Oriental*
Food Court (407) 851-1334

ORLANDO (Sanford), FL

American Grill *Fast Food*
Food Court

American Grill *Fast Food*

15 Best Airport Restaurants

Food Court

Blue Sky Express Food Court	*Fast Food*
Blue Sky Spirits Food Court	*Bar*
Budweiser Tap Room Food Court	*Bar*
Cafe Ritazza Food Court	*Italian*

PENSACOLA, FL

Varona's Lobby Gate 2	*Italian*

PHILADELPHIA, PA

Au Bon Pain Terminal C Gate 16	*Deli* 215-365-6160
Auntie Anne's Terminal B Gate 3	*Snacks* 215-492-5537
Burger King Terminal E Gate 6 Terminal D Gate 4	*Fast Food* 215-492-2389 215-492-2386
Chick fil A Terminal B/C	*Fast Food* 215-365-2886
Famous King of Pizza Terminal D	*Italian* 215-365-5073
Independence Brew Pub Terminal B/C	*Bar* 215-863-2212
Jay's Pretzels Terminal D	*Snacks* 856-952-2103
Le Petite Bistro Terminal A	*Deli* 215-365-4842

15 Best Airport Restaurants

   Terminal D   215-365-4156
   Terminal C   215-492-8485

Mrs. Field's Cookies   *Desserts*
   Terminal B Gate 3   215-937-0465

Philly Pretzels   *Snacks*
   Terminal C   215-937-0225

Sbarro Italian Eatery   *Italian*
   Terminal B/C Food Court   215-863-2252
   Terminal C Gate 23   215-937-0559
   Terminal F Gate 11   215-365-3622

Shades of Blue Lounge   *Bar*
   Terminal A Gate 22   215-492-4812

TGI Fridays   *American*
   Terminal B/C   215-365-4300

Yummy Pretzels   *Snacks*
   Terminal A   215-768-8278
   Terminal E   215-768-8278
   Terminal F   215-768-8278

PHOENIX, AZ

12th Fairway Bar and Grill   *Bar*
   Terminal 4

Blue Burrito   *Mexican*
   Terminal 3
   Terminal 4

Burger King   *Fast Food*
   Terminal 4

California Pizza Kitchen   *American*
   Terminal 4

Carvel Ice Cream   *Desserts*
   Terminal 3
   Terminal 4

Chili's Too   *American*
   Terminal 4

15 Best Airport Restaurants

Cinnabon *Desserts*
  Terminal 3
  Terminal 4

Cold Stone Creamery *Desserts*
  Terminal 4

Desert Springs Brewing Company *Bar*
  Terminal 4

Dick Clark's American Bandstand *Grill American*
  Terminal 3

Einstein Bagels *Deli*
  Terminal 4

El Bravo *Mexican*
  Terminal 4

Famous Famiglia Pizzeria *Italian*
  Terminal 4

Flo's Shanghai Cafe *Oriental*
  Terminal 4

Fox Sports Bar *Bar*
  Terminal 4

Fruithead Smoothies *Snacks*
  Terminal 4

Great Steak and Potato Co *American*
  Terminal 4

Home Turf Bar *Bar*
  Terminal 4

Jackalope Flats Bar *Bar*
  Terminal 3
  Terminal 4

Jake's Coffee House *Coffee*
  Terminal 2

JD Hogg's *American*
  Terminal 3

Jodi Maroni's *Italian*

15 Best Airport Restaurants

Terminal 4

Juice Works *Snacks*
Terminal 4

Kokopeli Deli *Deli*
Terminal 3
Terminal 4

Martini Bistro *Bar*
Terminal 4

Nathan's Hot Dog *Fast Food*
Terminal 4

Oaxaca *Mexican*
Terminal 4

Paradise Bakery and Cafe *Deli*
Terminal 4

Phoenix All Star Sports Bar *Bar*
Terminal 2

Pizza Hut *Italian*
Terminal 4

Pretzel Mania *Snacks*
Terminal 4

Quizno's *Fast Food*
Terminal 4

Roadhouse 66 Bar *Bar*
Terminal 4

Sbarro *Italian*
Terminal 3

Starbucks *Coffee*
Terminal 3
Terminal 4

Taberna del Tequila *Mexican*
Terminal 3
Terminal 4

TCBY *Desserts*

15 Best Airport Restaurants

Terminal 4

Vienna Beef Hot Dog   *Fast Food*
Terminal 3

Vit's Grab n Go   *Italian*
Terminal 2

Wendy's *Fast*   *Food*
Terminal 3
Terminal 4

Yoshi's Asian Grill   *Oriental*
Terminal 4

PITTSBURGH, PA

Au Bon Pain   *Deli*
Terminal D

Auntie Anne's Pretzels   *Snacks*
Terminal A
Terminal B

Ben and Jerry's   *Desserts*
Terminal Core
Terminal B

Charley's Steakery   *American*
Terminal A
Terminal B

City of Bridges Cafe   *American*
Terminal Landside

Fat Tuesday   *American*
Terminal B

Garden Gazebo   *American*
Terminal Core

Great Steak and Potato   *American*
Terminal Core

Madison Avenue Deli   *Deli*
Terminal Core
Terminal A

15 Best Airport Restaurants

Mayorga Coffee Roasters   *Coffee*
    Terminal A
    Terminal B
    Terminal Core

McDonald's   *Fast Food*
    Terminal B
    Terminal Core

O'Brien's Grille and Pub   *Bar*
    Terminal Core

Quaker Steak and Lube   *American*
    Terminal A

Ranch 1   *American*
    Terminal Core

Samuel Adams Brewhouse   *Bar*
    Terminal B
    Terminal C

Sbarro   *Italian*
    Terminal Core

TGI Fridays   *American*
    Terminal A
    Terminal D
    Terminal Core

Villa Pizza   *Italian*
    Terminal B

PORTLAND, OR

Beaverton Bakery   *Bakery*
    Oregon Market   503.281.3373

Capers Cafe   *Regional*
    South Lobby   503.280.1010

Coffee People   *American*
    Oregon Market   503.969.6417
    Terminal B   503.969.6417
    Terminal C   503.969.6417

15 Best Airport Restaurants

Cool Temptations
  Terminal C

Desserts
503.249.1679

Good Dog Bad Dog
  Terminal C
  Terminal D

Fast Food
503.281.2344
503.281.2344

Gustav's Pub and Grill
  Terminal C

Deli
503.284.4621

Jamba Juice
  Oregon Market

Healthy

Laurelwood Brewing Co
  Terminal A
  Terminal E

Bar

Panda Express
  Oregon Market

Oriental
503.335.9860

Pizza Schmizza
  Terminal C

Italian
503.281.2339

Pizzicato
  Oregon Market

Italian
503.284.4872

Quizno's Subs
  Oregon Market

Deli
503.282.6865

Riverfront Cafe
  Terminal C

American
503.288.0075

Rogue Ales Public House
  Terminal D

Bar
503.282.2630

Rose City Wine Bar
  Oregon Market

Bar
503.335.8385

Roses Restaurant and Bakery
  Terminal D

American

Sandoval's Fresh Mexican Grill
  Terminal C
  Oregon Market

Mexican
503.280.7707
503.280.7707

Stanford's Restaurant and Bar
  Oregon Market

American
503.493.4056

15 Best Airport Restaurants

Starbucks *Coffee*
　Terminal A
　Terminal D
　Baggage Claim
　South Lobby

Wendy's *Fast Food*
　Oregon Market
　Terminal C
　Terminal D

PROVIDENCE, RI

Block Island Bar and Cafe *Seafood*
　Terminal South Gate 7

Dunkin Donuts *Bakery*
　Terminal North Gate 14

TGI Fridays *American*
　Terminal North Gate 16

The Federal Tavern *American*
　Main Terminal

Tito's Cantina *Mexican*
　Terminal North Gate 10

Wolfgang Puck Kiosk *American*
　Terminal North
　Terminal South

RALEIGH/DURHAM, NC

AJ's Tavern *American*
　Terminal A (919) 840-0506

A&W *Fast Food*
　Terminal A (919) 840-0506
　Terminal C (919) 840-0506

Carolina Varsity Bar and Grill *Bar*
　Terminal A (919) 840-0506

Crosswinds Cafe *American*
　General Aviation (919) 840-7625

15 Best Airport Restaurants

Fresh Attractions
   Terminal A

Healthy
(919) 840-0506

Godfather's Pizza
   Terminal A

Italian
(919) 840-0506

Golden Corral Airport Express
   Terminal A

American
(919) 840-0506

Great American Bagel
   Terminal A
   Terminal C

Bakery
(919) 840-0506
(919) 840-0506

Green Leaf's
   Terminal A

Healthy
(919) 840-0506

Jersey Mike's
   Terminal A

Deli
(919) 840-3693

JQ Snacks
   Terminal A

Snacks
(919) 840-7631

Maui Taco
   Terminal C

Mexican
(919) 840-0089

Pinehurst Village Brewery
   Terminal C

Bar
(919) 840-0462

Popeye's
   Terminal A

Fast Food
(919) 840-0506

Sheetz
   Near Park & Ride Gate 3

Deli
(919) 840-0466

Starbucks
   Terminal A

Coffee
(919) 840-0506

Triangle Cyber Cafe
   Terminal C

Deli
(919) 840-3677

Wolfgang Puck to go
   Terminal A

American
(919) 840-0506

RENO, NV
Brew Brothers

Coffee

15 Best Airport Restaurants

Terminal Gaming

Esthel M Chocolates *Desserts*
Terminal Gaming Gate

M and M Stand *Snacks*
Terminal B Gate 1

McDonald's *Fast Food*
Terminal Gaming Gate

Munchito's *Mexican*
Terminal Gaming

Ritazza Coffee *Coffee*
Terminal B Gate 4

Tahoe Bar and Grill *Bar*
Terminal B Gate 6
Terminal Gaming

RICHMOND, VA

Applebee's *American*
Lobby Atrium

Caribou Coffee *Coffee*
Terminal A Atrium

Cheeburger Cheeburger *Fast Food*
Terminal B

Double T's *Regional*
Lobby Atrium

Sam Adams *Bar*
Terminal A
Terminal B

Vito's Market *Deli*
Terminal A

ROCHESTER, NY

Euro Cafe *Deli*
Terminal

15 Best Airport Restaurants

Famous Famiglia — *Italian*
Terminal

JW Dundee's Pub and Alehouse — *Bar*
Terminal

Keuka Sandwich and Salad Company — *Deli*
Terminal

McDonald's — *Fast Food*
Terminal

Players Sports Bar — *Bar*
Terminal

Red Osier — *Fast Food*
Terminal

Subway — *Deli*
Terminal

SACRAMENTO, CA

Burger King — *Fast Food*
Terminal A Food Court

California Pizza Kitchen — *American*
Terminal A Food Court

Capitol Burger Bar — *American*
Terminal A Food Court

Chilli's Too — *American*
Terminal B Food Court

Cinnabon — *Bakery*
Terminal A Food Court
Terminal A Baggage
Terminal B1 Ticketing

Gordon Beirsch — *American*
Terminal B2 Gate 24

Home Turf Sports Grill — *American*
Terminal A Gate 13

15 Best Airport Restaurants

Java City — *Coffee*
  Terminal A Gate 16
  Terminal B1 Gate 16

Juice — *Healthy*
  Terminal A Food Court
  Terminal B1 Ticketing

LA Salsa — *Mexican*
  Terminal A Food Court

Manchu Wok — *Oriental*
  Terminal A Food Court

Prospectors Pub — *Bar*
  Terminal A Food Court

Pyramid — *Regional*
  Terminal B Food Court

Starbucks — *Coffee*
  Terminal A Food Court
  Terminal A Gate Baggage
  Terminal B Food Court

TCBY — *Desserts*
  Terminal A Food Court
  Terminal B1 Ticketing

Vino Volo — *Deli*
  Terminal A Food Court

ST. LOUIS, MO

B Lounge and Grill — *Bar*
  Terminal A Gate 3

Brews and Blues Bar — *Bar*
  Terminal Main Gate 7

Budweiser Stadium Club Bar and Grill — *Bar*
  Terminal C Gate 19

Burger King — *Fast Food*
  Terminal E Gate 6
  Terminal D Gate 3
  Terminal Main 17 Gate

15 Best Airport Restaurants

California Pizza Kitchen   *American*
   Terminal E Gate 5
   Terminal A Gate 2

Carvel Ice Cream   *Desserts*
   Terminal Main Gate 5

Cheers   *Bar*
   Terminal D Gate 5

Chili's Too   *American*
   Terminal C Gate 9
   Terminal E Gate 2

Cinnabon   *Desserts*
   Terminal D Gate 1

Gateway Deli   *Deli*
   Terminal B Gate 3
   Terminal D Gate 1

Great American Bagle   *Deli*
   Terminal E Gate 14
   Terminal Main Gate 9

Home Plate Sports Bar   *Bar*
   Terminal E Gate 13

Jose Cuervo Tequileria   *Mexican*
   Terminal C Gate 1

Manchu Wok   *Oriental*
   Terminal D Gate 4
   Terminal Main Gate 17

Pretzel Time   *Snacks*
   Terminal C Gate 13
   Terminal Main Gate 4

Raving Wraps   *Deli*
   Terminal C Gate 15

Rib Cafe   *American*
   Terminal Main Gate 14

Schlafly's Taproom   *Bar*
   Terminal B Gate 2

Starbucks   *Coffee*
    Terminal A Gate 7
    Terminal C Gate 2
    Terminal C Gate 10
    Terminal E Gate 4
    Terminal E Gate 8
    Terminal Main Gate 6

TCBY   *Desserts*
    Terminal C Gate 6
    Terminal E Gate 7

Wolfgang Puck   *American*
    Terminal C Gate 4

ST. PETERSBURG, FL

Palm Terrace Restaurant   *American*
    2nd Floor

Ponce de Leon Lounge   *Bar*
    2nd Floor

SALT LAKE CITY, UT

Blue Burrito Grill   *Mexican*
    Terminal B

Burger King   *Fast Food*
    Terminal 1
    Terminal 2

California Pizza Kitchen   *American*
    Terminal D

Cinnabon   *Desserts*
    Terminal 2
    Terminal International

City Deli   *Deli*
    Terminal 2

Dick Clark's American Bandstand Grill   *Fast Food*
    Terminal 2

15 Best Airport Restaurants

Finnegan's — *Bar*
    Terminal International

Granato's — *Italian*
    Terminal 1

Great American Bagel — *Snacks*
    Terminal B

Juice Works — *Snacks*
    Terminal 1
    Terminal 2
    Terminal B
    Terminal International
    Terminal C

Krispy Kreme — *Desserts*
    Terminal 2

Manchu Wok — *Oriental*
    Terminal International

Millcreek Coffee Roasters — *Coffee*
    Terminal International
    Terminal D

Pizza Hut — *Italian*
    Terminal 1
    Terminal B

Quizno's — *Deli*
    Terminal A
Terminal E

Sbarro's — *Italian*
    Terminal 2

Squatters — *American*
    Terminal C Gate 3

Starbucks — *Coffee*
    Terminal 1
    Terminal 2
    Terminal International
    Terminal B
    Terminal E

TCBY — *Desserts*

15 Best Airport Restaurants

Terminal 1
Terminal 2
Terminal B
Terminal C
Terminal International

The Grove *Snacks*
Terminal B
Terminal C
Terminal D

The Hive *Bar*
Terminal B

The Terrace *American*
Terminal 1

Wall Street Deli *Deli*
Terminal C

Wasatch Pub *Bar*
Terminal D Gate 6

Wolfgang Pucks Express *American*
Terminal C

Yovana *Snacks*
Terminal International
Terminal 2

SAN ANTONIO, TX

Alamo Books and Cafe **Coffee**
Terminal 2 FC 210-820-3045

Alamo City Microbrewery and Grill **Bar**
Terminal 1 South Gate

Alamo Extra Newsstands **Snacks**
Terminal 1 Gate 5 210-930-3205
Terminal 2 210-930-3205

Blimpie Subs and Salads **Deli**
Terminal 1 Gate 8 210-822-1833

Cinnabon **Bakery**
Terminal 2 Lobby 210-826-9727

15 Best Airport Restaurants

Creative Croissants
    Terminal 1 Gate 10

Fast Food
210-826-8030

Famous Famiglia
    Terminal 1 Gate 2

Italian
210-930-8847

Gervin's Sports Bar
    Terminal 1 Gate 4

Bar
210-826-3698

Las Palapas
    Terminal 1 Lobby

Mexican
210-826-7500

McDonald's
    Terminal 1 Gate 2
    Terminal 2 FC

Fast Food
210-805-0002
210-805-8882

Quizno's Subs
    Terminal 2 FC

Deli
210-824-2550

Raising Canes
    Terminal 1 Gate 10

Fast Food

Rosario's Cantina
    Terminal 2

Mexican
210-826-3282

Starbucks
    Terminal 1 Gate 2
    Terminal 2

Coffee
210-826-6088

Taste of Orient
    Terminal 2 FC

Oriental
210-821-6599

Tribute Sports Bar
    Terminal 2 FC

Bar
210-828-6263

SAN DIEGO, CA

America's Cup Snack Bar
    Terminal 2 Gate 26

Snacks

Arriba Margarita Bar
    Terminal 1 Food Court

Bar

Bloody Mary's
    Terminal 2 Gate 27

Bar

15 Best Airport Restaurants

Boudin Bakery *Deli*
   Terminal 1 Gate Food Court

California Pizza Kitchen *American*
   Terminal 2 Gate 35

Central Snack *Snacks*
   Terminal 1 Food Court

Chili's *American*
   Terminal 1 Gate 2

Cinnabon *Desserts*
   Terminal 1 Gate 3
   Terminal 2 Food Court

Commuter Cafe *American*
   Terminal Commuter Post Security

Cramer's Deli *Deli*
   Terminal 2 Gate 39

Home Turf *Bar*
   Terminal 2 Gate 41

Karl Strauss Bar *Bar*
   Terminal 1 Gate 2
   Terminal 2

Kassiana Coffee *Coffee*
   Terminal 2 Baggage

La Salsa *Mexican*
   Terminal 2 Food Court

McDonald's *Fast Food*
   Terminal 1 Food Court
   Terminal 2 Food Court
   Terminal 2 Gate 35

Naked Juice *Snacks*
   Terminal 2

Nathan's *Fast Food*
   Terminal 2 Gate 26

NFL Bar *Bar*
   Terminal 1 United

15 Best Airport Restaurants

NFL Snack Bar — *Snacks*
    Terminal 1 United

Pizza Hut — *Italian*
    Terminal 1 Gate 3
    Terminal 1 United
    Terminal 2 Gate 26

Pizzeria Uno — *Italian*
    Terminal 1 Southwest

Rubio's — *Mexican*
    Terminal 1 Food Court

San Diego Tap Room — *Bar*
    Terminal 1 Southwest

Starbucks — *Coffee*
    Terminal 1 Ticketing
    Terminal 1 Gate 10
    Terminal 1 Food Courts
    Terminal 1 United
    Terminal 2 Gate 30
    Terminal 2 Gate 35

Submarina — *Deli*
    Terminal 2 Food Court

TCBY — *Desserts*
    Terminal 1 Southwest
    Terminal 1 United
    Terminal 2 Gate 26

Top Gun Bar — *Bar*
    Terminal 1 Gate 3

SAN FRANCISCO, CA

Amoura Café — *Deli*
    International Terminal Gate A3
650-821-0320

Anchor Brewing Company — *Bar*
    Terminal 3 Gate 70
650-821-8911

15 Best Airport Restaurants

Andalé Mexican Restaurant   Mexican
    International Terminal, Boarding Gate G91   650-821-8201
    Terminal 1 Gates 20-36   650-821-8942
    Terminal 3 Gates 80-90   650-821-0620

Boudin's Bakery and Café   Deli
    Terminal 3 Gates 80-90   650-871-2515

Boule Café   Deli
    International Terminal Main Hall   650-821-6013

The Buena Vista Café   American
    Terminal 3 Gate 82   650-827-6626

Burger Joint   Fast Food
    International Terminal South Food   650-821-0582

Burger King   Fast Food
    Terminal 3 Gate 74   650-821-8966

Deli-Up Café   Deli
    International Terminal Gate G93   650-821-6000

Ebisu   Japanese
    International Terminal North Food   650-588-2549

Emporio Rulli   Italian Deli
    International Terminal Arrivals Lobby   650-821-0539
    International Terminal North Food Court   650-821-6940
    International Terminal South Food Court   650-821-6941

Emporio Rulli Gran Caffe   Italian
    Terminal 3 Gate 79   650-821-8345

Firewood Café   American
    International Terminal Gate A12   650-588-8464
    Terminal 1 Gates 40-48   650-821-8968
    Terminal 3 Gates 80-90   650-821-8956

Firewood Grill   American
    International Terminal Gate A1   650-821-0530
    International Terminal Main Hall   650-821-1111

Fung Lum   Chinese
    International Terminal North Food   650-821-8282
    Terminal 1 Gates 40-48   650-821-8181
    Terminal 3 Gates 80-90   650-821-8383

15 Best Airport Restaurants

Go Bistro
    Terminal 1 Gate 24

Bar
650-821-0523

Gordon Biersch
    Terminal 3 Gate 74

Bar
650-827-6635

Guava & Java
    Terminal 1 Gate 48
    Terminal 3 Gates 60-67

Deli/Coffee
650-821-1033
650-821-8096

Harbor Village Kitchen
    International Terminal South Food

Chinese
650-821-8983

Il Fornaio Caffe Del Mondo
    International Terminal Gate A11
    International Terminal Gate G99

Italian
650-821-6440
650-821-9443

Jalapeno Grill
    Terminal 3 Gates 60-67

Mexican
650-821-0575

Just Desserts
    Terminal 1 Gates 20-36
    Terminal 1 Gates 40-48
    Terminal 3 Gates 80-90

Desserts
650.821.8947

Klein's Deli and Coffee Bar
    Terminal 1 Gate 36
    Terminal 3 Gate 64

Coffee/Deli
650.821.9178
650.821.9179

Legends of San Francisco
    Terminal 1 Gate 31

Deli
650-821-0553

Lori's Diner
    International Terminal North Food
    Terminal 1 Gates 20-36
    Terminal 3 Gates 80-90

American
650-821-7400
650-821-0550
650-821-0500

Max's Eatz and Fresh Bakery
    Terminal 1 Gate 23

Deli
650-877-6632

Max's the Greek
    Terminal 3 Gates 70/71

Greek/Deli
650-827-6638

Mission Bar and Grill
    Terminal 3 Gate 64

Bar
650-821-8304

Osho Japanese Cuisine
    International Terminal South Food Court

Japanese
650-821-8218

15 Best Airport Restaurants

Peet's Coffee & Tea   Coffee
    Terminal 1 near International connector   650-821-8950
    Terminal 1 Gate 26   650-821-8952
    Terminal 3 Gates 70/71   650-821-8953
    Terminal 3 Gate 88   650-821-8955
    Terminal 3 Mezzanine Level Food Court   650-821-8951

Perry's   American
    Terminal 1 Gate 42   650-821-1037
    www.perryssf.com

San Francisco Soup Company   Healthy
    Terminal 3 Gates 80-90   650-821-7687

Sankaku   Japanese
    Terminal 3 Gates 70/71   650-821-0808

Soup and Salad Station   Healthy
    Terminal 3 Mezzanine Level Food Court   650-821-8965

Starbucks   Coffee
    Terminal 3 Arrivals Level   650-821-8753

Subway   Fast Food
    Terminal 3 Gates 60-67   650-821-8094
    Terminal 3 Mezzanine Level Food Court   650-821-1040

T.G.I. Friday's   American
    Terminal 1 Gates 20-36   650-821-8090

Tomokazu   Japanese
    International Terminal Gate G93   650-821-8899
    Terminal 3 Gates 80-90   650-821-8833

Willow Creek Grill   American
    Terminal 1 Gate 25   650-821-1117
    Terminal 3 Gates 70/71   650-821-8945

Willow Street Woodfired Pizza   Italian
    International Terminal Main Hall North Food   650-589-3978

Yankee Pier   Seafood
    Terminal 3 Gate 72   650-821-8938
    www.yankeepier.com

SAN JOSE, CA

Bits and Bytes — *Snacks*
Terminal C Gate FC

Burger King — *Fast Food*
Terminal A Gate 5
Terminal C Gate FC

California Pizza Kitchen — *American*
Terminal A Gate 5

Cinnabon — *Bakery*
Terminal A Gate 5

Freshens — *Healthy*
Terminal A Gate 5

Gordon Biersch — *American*
Terminal A Gate 5

Grab n Go — *Snacks*
Terminal C Gate FC

Harbor Express — *Fast Food*
Terminal C Gate FC

Martini Monkey — *Bar*
Terminal C Gate 11

Max's San Jose — *American*
Terminal A Gate 11

Noah's Bagels — *American*
Terminal C Gate 1

Runways — *American*
Terminal C Gate 6

Sr. Jalapeño — *Mexican*
Terminal C Gate FC

Starbucks — *Coffee*
Terminal A Gate 7
Terminal A Gate 3
Terminal C Gate FC

SANTA ANA, CA

Brioche Doree Cafe and Bakery *American*
Terminal A/B Food Court

Creative Croissants *Fast Food*
Terminal B

Gibson Guitar Lounge *Bar*
Terminal A (949) 252-6125

McDonald's *Fast Food*
Terminal A

Oasis Grill and Sky Lounge *American*
Terminal A/B Food Court

Quick Connection Food Service *Fast Food*
Terminal A Gate 14
Terminal B Gate 1

Sports Page Pub *Bar*
Terminal B

Starbucks *Coffee*
Terminal A
Terminal B
Terminal A/B Food Court

SANTA BARBARA, CA

Creative Croissants *Deli*
Terminal Lobby Downstairs

Overlook Cafe *American*
Terminal Lobby Upstairs

SARASOTA, FL

Bayfront Restaurant and Lounge *American*
Terminal Main 2nd Floor

Budweiser Brewhouse *Bar*
Terminal Main FC

15 Best Airport Restaurants

Fresh Attractions *Healthy*
    Terminal Main 2nd Floor

Gourmet Bean *Coffee*
    Terminal Main 2nd Floor

High Tides Deli and Lounge *American*
    Main Terminal

Wolfgang Puck *American*
    Main Terminal

SAVANNAH, GA

Budweiser Brew Pub *Bar*
    Terminal

Burger King *Fast Food*
    Terminal FC

Dewar's Clubhouse Bar and Grille *Bar*
    Terminal FC

Nathan's *Fast Food*
    Terminal FC

Phillip's Famous Seafood *American*
    Terminal

Pizza Hut *Italian*
    Terminal FC

Starbucks *Coffee*
    Terminal

TCBY *Desserts*
    Terminal FC

Wolfgang Pucks *American*
    Terminal

SEATTLE, WA

Africa Lounge *Bar*
    Terminal Central Gate

15 Best Airport Restaurants

Alaska Lodge — *American*
    Terminal C Gate C1

Anchor Brewing Company — *Bar*
    Terminal 3F Gate 69

Andale — *Mexican*
    Terminal 3F Gate Food Court
    Terminal 1B Gate Food Court
    Terminal International Gate G91

Anthony's — *American*
    Terminal Central Gate

Botanical Tea Infusion — *Deli*
    Terminal South Sat Gate Food Court

Burger King — *Fast Food*
    Terminal D Gate D5 & D6
    Terminal North Sate Gate Food Court
    Terminal South Sat Gate Food Court

Carry Out Carry On — *Deli*
    Terminal D Gate D7

Casa del Agave — *Mexican*
    Terminal B Gate 4

Cascade Lounge — *Bar*
    Terminal South Sat Food Court

Chili's Too — *American*
    Terminal D Gate 12

Dreyer's Ice Cream — *Desserts*
    Terminal North Sat Gate N1

Freshen's — *American*
    Terminal D Gate D6

Glacier River Cafe — *American*
    Terminal B Gate B4 & B6

Ivar's Seafood Bar — *Seafood*
    Terminal Central Gate

Jonathan's Cocktails and Snacks — *Bar*
    Terminal D Gate D7

15 Best Airport Restaurants

Kathy Casey Dish D'Lish *Fast Food*
    Terminal Central Gate
    Terminal Main Gate

La Pisa Cafe *Italian*
    Terminal A Gate A9
    Terminal C Gate C12

Maki of Japan *Oriental*
    Terminal Central Gate

Manchu Wok *Oriental*
    Terminal A Gate A5

Old Seattle Deli *Deli*
    Terminal D Gate 12

Pallino Pastaria *Italian*
    Terminal Central Gate

Pilot House *American*
    Terminal Main Gate

Qdoba Mexican Grill *Mexican*
    Terminal Central Gate

Runway Deli *Deli*
    Terminal South Sat Gate Food Court

Sbarro *Deli*
    Terminal B Gate B3

Seattle Tap Room *Bar*
    Terminal B Gate B1

Seattle's Best Coffee *Coffee*
    Terminal D Gate D6
    Terminal South Sat Gate S1

See's Candy *Desserts*
    Terminal North Sat Gate N1

Sports Page Pub *Bar*
Terminal D Gate D3

Starbucks *Coffee*
    Terminal B Gate B3

15 Best Airport Restaurants

Terminal B Gate B10
Terminal C Gate C9
Terminal North Sat Gate N10

Tequileria *Mexican*
Terminal B Gate B4

The Edge Sports Bar *Bar*
Terminal North Sat Food Court

The Great American Bagel Bakery *Deli*
Terminal A Gate 5
Terminal D Gate D5
Terminal North Sat Food Court

The Mountain Room Bar *Bar*
Terminal A Gate 14

Tully's Coffee *Coffee*
Terminal A Gate A9

Udon Station *Deli*
Terminal South Sat Food Court

Vino Volo *American*
Terminal Central Gate

Waji's *Oriental*
Terminal C Gate 12

Wolfgang Puck *American*
Terminal C Gate 10

SOUTH BEND, IN

Air Host Coffee *Coffee*
East End

Cafe SBN *American*
West End (574) 289-8786

TALLAHASSEE, FL

All American Grille *American*
Main Terminal FC

15 Best Airport Restaurants

Caffe Ritazza — Italian
  Main Terminal FC

Capital City Grill — American
  Lobby

Creative Croissants — Deli
  Main Terminal FC

Freshens — Healthy
  Main Terminal FC

Outtakes — Deli
  Lobby

Samuel Adams — Bar
  Terminal Lobby Gate

Tipperary's Irish Pub — Bar
  Main Terminal FC

Uno Chicago Pizza — Italian
  Main Terminal FC

TAMPA, FL

Burger King — Fast Food
  Landside

Cafe Elise — American
  Marriot Hotel

Casa Bacardi — Mexican
  Airside E Gate 68

Chick fil A — Fast Food
  Airside F Gate 85

Chilli's Too — American
  Airside F

Chill's Too — American
  Airside C Gate 31

Da Vincis Cafe — Italian
  Airside E Gate 69

15 Best Airport Restaurants

Edy's Ice Cream   *Desserts*
   Landside

Flatbreadz   *Italian*
   Airside F Gate 85

Frankly Gourmet   *Fast Food*
   Airside E Gate 64

Frankly Gourmet   *Fast Food*
   Airside F Gate 85

Home Team   *Bar*
   Airside C Gate 39

Jose Cuervo's   *Mexican*
   Airside A Gate 12

Nathan's   *Deli*
   Airside C Gate 36

Pizza Hut   *Italian*
   Landside
   Airside A Gate 12

Quizno's   *Deli*
   Airside A Gate 12
   Airside C Gate 42

Skyye Lounge   *Bar*
   Marriot Hotel

Starbucks   *Coffee*
   Landside
   Marriott Hotel
   Airside A Gate 12
   Airside C Gate 36
   Airside E Gate 69
   Airside F Gate 85

Taco Bell Express   *Fast Food*
   Landside

TGI Friday's   *American*
   Landside

The View at CK's   *American*
   Marriot Hotel

15 Best Airport Restaurants

Wall Street Deli — *Deli*
Landside

Wharf Grill and Brewhouse — *American*
Landside

TULSA, OK

Camille's Sidewalk Cafe — *American*
Terminal A Gate 27

Cherry Street Cafe — *American*
Terminal Pre-Security

Freckles Frozen Custard — *Desserts*
Food Court

Java Dave's — *Coffee*
Terminal A Gate 28

Mazzio's Pizza — *Italian*
Food Court

Quizno's — *Deli*
Food Court

Starbuck's — *Coffee*
Food Court

TGI Friday's — *American*
Terminal A Gate 21

Varsity Grill and Sports Bar — *Bar*
Terminal A Gate 56

TUCSON, AZ

Arizona Sports Grill *American*
Terminal A FC

Boars Head Deli — *Deli*
Terminal A FC
Terminal B FC

Carmella's Kitchen Gourmet Pizza — *Italian*

15 Best Airport Restaurants

Terminal B FC

Cheeburger Cheeburger — *American*
Terminal A FC

Cibo Express Gourmet Market — *Deli*
Terminal A FC
Terminal B FC

Ike's Coffee Bar and Cocktails — *Bar*
Terminal A FC
Terminal B FC

Jet Rock Cafe — *American*
Terminal A/B 3rd Floor

Sky Asian Bistro — *Oriental*
Terminal B FC

Taco Bron — *Mexican*
Terminal A FC

WASHINGTON (Dulles), DC

Auntie Anne's — *Snacks*
Terminal C Gate 11
703-572-5200

Ben and Jerry's Ice Cream — *Desserts*
Terminal B Gate 23
703-572-2516

California Tortilla — *Mexican*
Terminal C Gate 22
703-572-7333

Caribou Coffee — *Coffee*
Terminal Main
703-572-3368

Cinnabon — *Desserts*
Terminal Main
703-572-1853

Cosi — *Italian*
Terminal A Gate 7
703-572-3360

Cuisine D Avion — *Deli*
Terminal Main
703-572-6705
Terminal D Gate 24
703-661-4611

Dunkin Donuts — *Desserts*

15 Best Airport Restaurants

    Terminal B Gate 22   703-572-6845
    Terminal D Gate 5   703-572-6895

Euro Cafe   *Deli*
    Terminal A Gate 4   703-572-7351

Famous Famiglia   *Italian*
    Terminal A Gate 4   703-572-5203

Firkin and Fox   *Bar*
    Terminal C Gate 22   703 -661-5001

Five Guys   *Fast Food*
    Terminal A Gate 3   703-661-8787

Fuddrucker's   *Fast Food*
    Terminal B Gate 22   703-572-6275

Gas Light Bakery   *Deli*
    Terminal B Gate Center   703-661-6653

Gordon Biersch   *Bar*
    Terminal D Gate 14   703-572-4701

Guava and Java   *Coffee*
    Terminal Baggage Gate 3   703-572-6336

Harry's Tap Room   *Bar*
    Terminal B Gate 41   703-661-0963
    Terminal Main   703-661-2164

Jose Cuervo Tequileria   *Mexican*
    Terminal B Gate 38   703 572-4702

Matsutake Sushi   *Oriental*
    Terminal B Gate 23   703-572-6438

Maui Wowi Hawaiian Coffees and Smoothies   *Coffee*
    Terminal C Gate 9   703-572-6637
    Terminal C Gate 28   703-572-6637

Mayorga Coffee   *Coffee*
    Terminal A Gate 3   703-5725131

Moe's Grill and Bar   *American*
    Terminal D Gate 19   703 661-6980

Nelson's Food and Spirits   *American*

15 Best Airport Restaurants

    Terminal D Gate 24   703 572-6278

Old Dominion Brewing Co.   *American*
    Terminal B Gate 19   703-572-6875

Potbelly Sandwich Works   *Fast Food*
    Terminal B Gate 48   703-572-6369
    Terminal C Gate 2   703-572-6385

Starbuck's *Coffee*
    Terminal Baggage   703-572-4616
    Terminal C Gate 7   703-572-4614
    Terminal B Gate 47   703-572-6874
    Terminal C Gate 24   703-572-4613
    Terminal D Gate 16   703-572-2686

Subway *Fast Food*
    Terminal D Gate 14   703-572-6901
    Terminal Main   703-572-5217

Tidewater Landing   *American*
    Terminal C Gate 11   703-572-3325

Villa Pizza   *Italian*
    Terminal B Gate 23   703-572-5120
    Terminal D Gate 23   703-572-5123

Vino Volo Wine Room   *Italian*
    Terminal C Gate 3   703-661-1999

Wendy's   *Fast food*
    Terminal C Gate 21   703-661-6760

WASHINGTON (Reagan), DC

Allie's Deli   *Deli*
    Terminal A Gate

Auntie Anne's Soft Pretzels   *Snacks*
    Center Pier   (703) 417-1755
    North Pier   (703) 417-8316

Carmella's Kitchen   *Italian*
    Hall   (703) 417-1980
    Hall   (703) 417-1980

Cibo Bistro and Wine Bar   *Bar*

15 Best Airport Restaurants

Hall	(703) 417-1980
Cinnabon	*Desserts*
North Pier	(703) 417-1654
Cosi	*Deli*
Hall	(703) 417-4430
DC Samuel Adams	*Bar*
Terminal A	(703) 417-1706
DCA Bar and Grill	*Bar*
Terminal Connector	(703) 417-0690
Dunkin Donuts	*Desserts*
North Pier	(703) 418-0631
Center Pie	(703) 418-0630
Einstein Bros Bagels	*Snacks*
South Pier	(703) 417-1624
Famous Famiglia	*Italian*
Center Pier	(703) 417-1622
Five Guys	*Fast Food*
North Pier	(703) 417-1990
Freshen's	*Desserts*
North Pier	(703) 417-1962
Fuddrucker's	*Fast Food*
Center Pier	(703) 417-3018
Gordon Biersch	*Bar*
North Pier	(703) 417-1001
Illy's Coffee	*Coffee*
North Hall	(703) 417-1983
Jerry's Subs and Pizza	*Italian*
Terminal A	(703) 417-1709
Legal Sea Foods	*American*
North Hall	(703) 413-9810
Mamma Ilardo's Pizzeria	*Italian*
North Pier	(703) 417-1962

15 Best Airport Restaurants

Matsutake Sushi
Center Hall

Oriental
(703) 417-0521

Mayorga Coffee Roasters
South Pier

Coffee
(703) 417-0652

Panda Express
Center Pier

Oriental
(703) 412-9169

Potbelly Sandwich Works
Center Pier

Deli
(703) 417-3092

Primo Cappuccino
North Pier

Coffee
(703) 417-1830

Ranch 1
North Pier

Fast Food

Sam's Brewhouse
Center Pier

Bar
(703) 417-0066

Samuel Adams Brewhouse
Terminal A

Bar
(703) 417-8557

Starbucks
Terminal A

Coffee
(703) 417-0808

TGI Friday's
Center Pier

American
(703) 417-1900

Tidewater Landing
South Pier

American
(703) 417-0501

WEST PALM BEACH, FL

Burger King
Terminal B
Terminal A

Fast Food

California Pizza Kitchen ASAP
Terminal Main Level 2

American

Cinnabon
Terminal Main Level 2

Bakery

Hoffman's
Terminal B

Desserts

15 Best Airport Restaurants

Miami Subs Grill and Bar   *Fast Food*
    Terminal C

Nick's Tomatoe Pie   *Italian*
    Terminal A
    Terminal B
    Terminal C

Rooney's Public House   *American*
    Terminal Main Level 2

Sam Snead's Tavern   *American*
    Terminal Main

Starbucks   *Coffee*
    Terminal Main Level 2
    Terminal A
    Terminal B
    Terminal B
    Terminal C
    Terminal Main

TCBY   *Desserts*
    Terminal B

WICHITA, KS

Air Capital Bar   *Bar*
    East Concourse Gate 3

Burger King   *Fast Food*
    Ground Level

Fast Break Bar   *Bar*
    West Concourse Gate 10

Fresh Attractions   *Deli*
    Ground Level

Great American Bagel   *Bakery*
    East Concourse Gate 3
    West Concourse Gate 10

Hot Dog City   *Fast Food*
    Ground Level

15 Best Airport Restaurants

Pizza Hut *Italian*
Ground Level

Sarah's Ice Cream and Cookies *Desserts*
Ground Level

Sweet Treat *Desserts*
Ground Level

The Landing *American*
Ground Level

Waffle Bar *Bakery*
Ground Level

WINDSOR LOCKS, CT

Boston Pizza *Italian*
Terminal A Food Court

Concordes Restaurant *American*
Sheraton Hotel

Edy's *Desserts*
Terminal A

Einstein's Bagels *Deli*
Terminal A

Fresh City *Snacks*
Terminal A Food Court

Fresh Soft Beforetzels *Snacks*
Terminal A Food Court

Island Oasis Smoothies *Snacks*
Terminal A Food Court

Last Resort Lounge *Bar*
Terminal A

LavAzza Coffee and Pastry *Coffee*
Terminal A

Locks Landing *Deli*
Terminal A

15 Best Airport Restaurants

McDonald's *Fast Food*
    Terminal A Food Court

Starbucks *Coffee*
    Sheraton Lobby

Sundowner Cafe *American*
    Terminal B

Wicked Good Subs *Deli*
    Terminal A

Made in the USA
Coppell, TX
26 July 2023

19610449R00079